**This book is to be returned on or before
the last date stamped below.**

Timothy O'Neill
MERCHANTS AND MARINERS

IRELAND

ATLANTIC
OCEAN

IRISH
SEA

Aranmore
Is.
Carrickfergus
Copeland
Is.
Donegal
LOUGH
NEAGH
Ardglass
BALLYSHANNON
BAY
ERNE
Sligo
Carlingford
Dundalk
Clogherhead
Athboy
Drogheda
Roscommon
Navan
Skerries
Trim
ACHILL
Is
CLEW
BAY
Lambay Is
Malahide
LOUGH
CORRIB
Athlone
Howth
Dublin
Dalkey
Galway
Athenry
Aran
Is
Wicklow
Carlow
Limerick
Holycross
Kilkenny
Thomastown
Cashel
New Ross
Carrigafoyle
Clonmel
Wexford
Waterford
Tuscar
Rock
Hook Head
Dingle
Blasket
Is
Cork
Youghal
N
Kinsale
KENMARE R.
Dursey Is
Baltimore
0   10   20   30
Cape Clear
Miles

Timothy O'Neill

MERCHANTS
AND
MARINERS
in Medieval Ireland

IRISH ACADEMIC PRESS

The typesetting of this book was input by
Gilbert Gough Typesetting, Dublin
in 11 on 12 point Plantin
and was output by
Computer Graphics Ltd, Dublin
for Irish Academic Press, Kill Lane, Blackrock, Co. Dublin.

Printed in Great Britain by
St Edmundsbury Press,
Bury St Edmunds, Suffolk, England.

BRITISH LIBRARY CATALOGUING IN PUBLICATION DATA

O'Neill, Timothy
Merchants and mariners in medieval Ireland.
1. Ireland — Economic conditions
I. Title
330.9415   HC260.5

ISBN 0-7165-2398-1
ISBN 0-7165-2399-X Pbk

I ndil chuimhne ar
mo thuismitheoirí
Peggy & Owen O'Neill
+ 1985

Contents

List of maps and illustrations   8

Preface   9

Acknowledgements   10

Abbreviations   11

INTRODUCTION The sources   15

I FOOD AND DRINK   20
   Corngrowing and the grain trade   20
   The fish trade   30
   The wine trade   44

II CLOTHING   58
   Wool production and marketing   58
   Cloth production and exports   65
   The importation of English cloth   70
   Trade in cow hides and calf skins   77

III MINERALS AND STONE   84
   Salt and iron from Brittany and Spain   84
   Millstones and building stone   92

IV LUXURY IMPORTS AND MISCELLANEOUS
   EXPORTS   94

V SHIPS AND MARINERS   107
   Types of trading and fishing vessels   107
   Navigation and sea-charts   113
   Piracy off the Irish coasts   119

CONCLUSION   130

Notes and References   132

Bibliography   149

Index   161

Maps and Illustrations

Ireland   *Frontispiece*

1 Carrickfergus, a sixteenth century drawing   25
2 Cork, *c.* 1600   26
3 Fishing in the Irish Sea, *c.* 1580   33
4 Carrigafoyle castle, Co. Kerry   35
5 Ross Errilly friary, Co. Galway   36
6 Galway, *c.* 1600   42
7 Limerick, *c.* 1600   49
8 Dublin, *c.* 1600   53
9 Cloth seal, bearing the arms of Rouen, *c.* 1500   64
10 The Irish mantle   69
11 The mayors of Dublin, Waterford, Cork and Limerick   73
12 Ireland, 1339 by Angelino Dulcert   81
13 Western Europe   83
14 The overseas trade of Drogheda xiii-xv centuries   87
15 Timber-framed house, Dublin   89
16 Monks singing, fourteenth century illustration   97
17 Timber-framed house, Drogheda   101
18 A king with a falcon   102
19 Art Mac Murchadha, 1399   105
20 Noah's Ark, Book of Ballymote   107
21 Municipal seal of Youghal, 1527   108
22 Warships, from John Goghe's Map of Ireland, 1567   110
23 Caravel from John Goghe's Map   111
24 Ireland, *c.* 1450, from the Upsal map   115
25 Michael Tregury, archbishop of Dublin, 1449-71   117
26 Drogheda, 1657   123
27 A naval battle, Holinshead's *Irish Chronicle*, 1577   125
28 Kinsale Harbour, 1587   127

Preface

My thanks are due in the first place to Rev. Professor F. X. Martin, OSA, who encouraged my interest in fourteenth- and fifteenth-century Irish history and who directed my attention to the topic of trade. I owe much to the scholarship of Dr H. B. Clarke, who supervised my initial research and more recently read the typescript of this book and made many helpful suggestions. I benefitted greatly from the advice and the research of Dr Wendy Childs, with whom I worked on a joint contribution to *A New History of Ireland* and I record my thanks to the editors and contributors for allowing me to use material soon to be published. My friends, Anthony Lynch and John Bradley also helped with ideas and references.

I am grateful to the librarians and archivists of The Library, Trinity College, Dublin; the Public Record Office of Ireland; the National Library of Ireland; St Peter's College, Wexford; and particularly Mrs Brigid Dolan and her staff at the library of the Royal Irish Academy, Dublin. I thank Brigit Murphy and June O'Connor who typed the manuscript and Michael Adams of Irish Academic Press for undertaking to publish the work.

Finally, I am grateful to the members of my community, the De La Salle Brothers, for allowing me to take a sabbatical from teaching in order to write the book, and my friends in Caherdaniel whose encouragement helped me to persevere at the task in the quiet of a west Kerry winter.

Tadhg Ó Néill,

CATHAIR DÓNALL, SAMHAIN 1986.

Acknowledgements

The author and publishers make grateful acknowledgement for the use of illustrations to the Irish Architectural Archive, Dublin, the National Library of Ireland; the National Museum of Ireland; the Public Record Office, London; the Royal Irish Academy; the Royal Society of Antiquaries of Ireland, John Bradley; P.F. Wallace; and Mrs. A.K. Leask.

Abbreviations

A.U.	*Annála Uladh: Annals of Ulster* ... *a chronicle of Irish Affairs from A.D. 431 to A.D. 1541* ed. W. M. Hennessy and B. MacCarthy (4 vols, Dublin, 1887-1901).
Account roll of Holy Trinity	*Account roll of the priory of the Holy Trinity, Dublin, 1337-1346,* ed. James Mills (Dublin, 1891).
Anal. Hib.	*Analecta Hibernica, including the reports of the Irish Manuscripts Commission* (Dublin, 1930-).
Anc. rec. Dublin.	*Calendar of ancient records of Dublin in the possession of the municipal corporation,* ed. Sir J. T. Gilbert and Lady Gilbert (19 vols, Dublin, 1889-1944).
Arthur MS	The Arthur Manuscript, ed. E. A. MacLysaght and John Ainsworth in *N. Munster Antiq. Jn.,* 8 (1958), pp 3-19.
Belfast Natur. Hist. Soc. Proc.	*Proceedings and Reports of the Belfast Natural History and Philosophical Society* (Belfast, 1873-).
Blake family records	*Blake family records, series i:* 1300-1600, ed. M. J. Blake (London, 1902).
Bolton, *English Economy*	J. L. Bolton, *The Medieval English Economy, 1150-1500* (London, 1980).
Cal. Carew MSS 1515-74 [etc.]	*Calendar of the Carew manuscripts preserved in the archiepiscopal library at Lambeth, 1515-74* [etc.] (6 vols, London, 1867-73).
Cal. close rolls, 1272-9 [etc.]	*Calendar of the close rolls,* 1272-9 [etc.] (London, 1900-)
Cal. doc. Ire., 1171-1251 [etc.]	*Calendar of the documents relating to Ireland, 1171-1251* [etc.] (5 vols, London, 1875-86).
Cal. pat. rolls, 1232-47 [etc.]	*Calendar of the patent rolls, 1232-47* [etc.] (London, 1906-).
Carus-Wilson, *Overseas trade of Bristol*	E. M. Carus-Wilson, *The overseas trade of Bristol in the later middle ages* (Bristol, 1937).

Cal. justic. rolls
Ire., 1295-1303)
[etc.]

Calendar of the justiciary rolls, or proceedings in the court of the justiciar of Ireland . . . 1295-1303 [etc.] ed. James Mills (2 vols, Dublin, 1905, 1914).

Chester Customs

Chester Customs Accounts 1301-1566 ed. K. P. Wilson (Liverpool, 1969).

Childs, 'Ireland's trade'

W. A. Childs, 'Ireland's trade with England in the later middle ages' in Ir. Econ. & Soc. Hist., ix (1982), pp 5-33.

Childs & O'Neill 'Overseas trade'

W. A. Childs and Timothy O'Neill, 'Overseas trade' in N.H.I., II, pp 492-524.

Cork Hist. Soc. Jn.

Journal of the Cork Historical and Archaeological Society (Cork, 1892-).

Facs. nat. MSS Ire.

Facsimiles of the national manuscripts of Ireland, ed. J. T. Gilbert (4 vols, Dublin, 1874-84).

Galway Archives Soc. Jn.

Archives of the town of Galway ed. J. T. Gilbert in Historical Manuscripts Commission Report 10, Appendix v (1885), pp 380-520.

Galway Arch. Soc. Jn.

Journal of the Galway Archaeological and Historical Society (Galway, 1900-).

Hore, Wexford town

P. H. Hore, History of the town and county of Wexford (6 vols, London, 1900-11).

I.H.S.

Irish Historical Studies: the joint journal of the Irish Historical Society and the Ulster Society for Irish Historical Studies (Dublin, 1938-).

I.M.C.

Irish Manuscripts Commission, Dublin.

Ir. Econ. & Soc. Hist.

Irish Economic and Social History: the journal of the Economic and Social History Society of Ireland (Dublin and Belfast, 1974-).

Longfield, Anglo-Irish trade

A. K. Longfield, Anglo-Irish trade in the sixteenth century (London, 1929).

Louth Arch. Soc. Jn.

Journal of the County Louth Archaeological Society (Dundalk, 1904-).

Lydon, Eng. and Ire.

J. F. Lydon, (ed.) England and Ireland in the later middle ages (Dublin, 1981).

Lydon, Lordship

J. F. Lydon, The lordship of Ireland in the middle ages (Dublin and London, 1972).

Lydon, 'Ireland's participation'

J. F. Lydon, 'Ireland's participation in the military activities of English kings in the thirteenth and early fourteenth century' (Ph.D. thesis, University of London, 1955).

MacNiocaill, Na Buirgéisí

Gearóid Mac Niocaill, Na Buirgéisí, xii-xv aois (2 vols, Dublin, 1964).

Maxwell, *Sources*	Constantia Maxwell, *Irish history from contemporary sources, 1509-1610* (London, 1923).
N.H.I.	A new history of Ireland (Oxford, 1976-) II (1987) Medieval Ireland, 1169-1534 ed. Art Cosgrove; III (1976), Early Modern Ireland 1534-1691, ed. T. W. Moody, F. X. Martin and F. J. Byrne.
N.L.I.	National Library of Ireland.
N. Munster Antiq. Jn.	*North Munster Antiquarian Journal* (Limerick, 1936-).
Nicholls, 'Gaelic Society'	Kenneth Nicholls, 'Gaelic Society and Economy in the high middle ages' in *N.H.I.* II, pp 397-438.
O'Flaherty, *West Connaught*	Roderick O'Flaherty, *A chorographical description of West or h-Iar Connaught, written A.D. 1684*, ed. James Hardiman (Ir. Arch. Soc., Dublin, 1846).
Ormond deeds, 1172-1350 [etc.]	*Calendar of Ormond deeds, 1172-1350* etc. Edmund Curtis (I.M.C., 6 vols, Dublin, 1932-43).
P.R.I. rep. D.K.I. [etc.]	First [etc.] *report of the deputy keeper of the public records in Ireland* (Dublin, 1869-).
P.R.O.	Public Record Office of England.
P.R.O.I.	Public Record Office of Ireland.
P.R.O.N.I.	Public Record Office of Northern Ireland.
Proc. king's council, Ire., 1392-3	*A roll of the proceedings of the king's council in Ireland for a portion of the sixteenth year of the reign of Richard II 1392-3*, ed. James Graves, (London, 1877).
R.I.A.	Royal Irish Academy.
R.I.A. Proc.	*Proceedings of the Royal Irish Academy* (Dublin, 1836-).
R.S.A.I. Jn.	*Journal of the Royal Society of Antiquaries of Ireland* (Dublin, 1892-).
Register of wills, ed. Berry	*Register of wills and inventories of the diocese of Dublin, in the time of Archbishops Tregury and Walton*, ed. H. F. Berry (Dublin, 1898).
Rot. pat. Hib.	*Rotulorum patentium et clausorum cancellariae Hiberniae calendarium*, ed. Edward Tresham (Dublin, 1828).
Stat. Ire., John-Hen. V	*Statutes and ordinances, and acts of the parliament of Ireland, King John to Henry V*, ed. H. F. Berry (Dublin, 1907).
Stat. Ire., Henry VI	*Statute rolls of the parliament of Ireland, reign of King Henry VI*, ed. H. F. Berry (Dublin, 1910).
Stat. Ire., 1-12 Edw IV	*Statute rolls of the parliament of Ireland, 1st to 12th years of the reign of King Edward IV*, ed. H. F. Berry (Dublin, 1914).

Stat. Ire., 12-22 *Edw* IV	*Statute rolls of the parliament of Ireland, 12th and 13th to the 21st and 22nd years of the reign of King Edward IV,* ed. James F. Morrissey, (Dublin, 1939).
Studies	*Studies: an Irish Quarterly Review* (Dublin, 1912-).
T.C.D.	Trinity College, Dublin.
Waterford Archives	Archives of the municipal corporation of Waterford ed. J. T. Gilbert in *Historical Manuscripts Commission Report 10,* Appendix v (1885), pp 265-339.
Wilson 'Port of Chester'	K. P. Wilson, 'The port of Chester in the later middle ages' (Ph.D. thesis, University of Liverpool, 1965).
Wood, 'Commercial Intercourse with Ireland'	Herbert Wood, 'Commercial Intercourse with Ireland in the middle ages' in *Studies,* iv (1915), pp 250-266.

Introduction

THE SOURCES

'That the history of medieval Ireland is imperfectly known arises not so much from the lack of material as from the imperfect exploitation of what is available'. Thus wrote H. G. Richardson and G. O. Sayles in 1961, adding 'that despite the disaster of 1922, there are few European countries that can command such a wealth of historical sources, as Ireland'. Aubrey Gwynn, however, was more pessimistic when referring to the economic history of medieval Ireland. He observed that 'there is an almost total lack of trustworthy materials, and of any serious critical work on the few materials that have come down to us'. Many of the contributions in *A New History of Ireland* Vol II (Medieval Ireland, 1169-1534) and this study of Irish trade reveal that the scene is not so bleak as Gwynn suggested but that, as Richardson and Sayles hinted, a considerable amount of material can be gleaned from a variety of sources. It was possible, in fact, to make a wide-ranging survey of medieval Irish imports and exports based largely on printed materials.

Among the richest sources of information for the medieval economic historian are port books and customs accounts, which record the arrivals and departures of ships and give details of their cargoes. Unfortunately no such records survive for any Irish port in the fourteenth or fifteenth century. Port books and customs accounts do exist for several English ports, including Bristol and Chester, both of which had close relations with Ireland. The port records yield invaluable information on Anglo-Irish trade. This was shown for the sixteenth century by A. K. Longfield, who based her study *Anglo-Irish trade in the sixteenth century* almost exclusively on port books and customs accounts. More recently, in 1981, similar sources have been expertly used by Wendy Childs in her comprehensive study 'Ireland's trade with England in the later middle ages'.*

*Publication details of all works cited in the introduction are given in the bibliography.

E. M. Carus-Wilson made a major contribution to the historiography of Bristol and was the author of *The overseas trade of Bristol in the later middle ages* — a collection of documents including a number of customs accounts translated and published in full, and of *Medieval Merchant Venturers* — a series of essays which contain further information on trade between Bristol and Ireland before 1500. One of the last articles she wrote, 'The overseas trade of late medieval Coventry', shows the close links between eastern Ireland and the city of Coventry. K. P. Wilson is the principal historian of medieval Chester. His unpublished Ph.D. thesis, 'The port of Chester in the later middle ages', is an analysis of the trade of the port and it contains a considerable amount of Irish material. He has also edited *Chester Customs Accounts 1301-1566*, a rich source for the history of medieval Irish trade.

In discussing the sources for the trade of medieval Bristol, Carus-Wilson remarked that, along with the customs accounts, the principal sources are the calendars of patent rolls and close rolls. These rolls record royal letters which were issued either open (letters patent) or closed (letters close). For the period 1300-1500, eighty-six volumes of calendars were examined. These, along with Edward Tresham's calendar of the patent and close rolls of the Irish chancery *Rotulorum Patentium et Clausorum cancellariae Hiberniae calendarium*, have supplied what proved to be the broad outlines of this survey. The numerous entries in the English calendars referring to Irish merchants and trade show clearly that Ireland figures in the economy of those areas of western Europe where English influence was felt. Tresham's calendar and the statute rolls of the Irish parliament (*c.* 1200-1483) give further details of the activities of Irish and foreign traders against the background of later medieval Ireland.

Possibly the greatest untapped source for medieval Irish history remains the memoranda rolls of the Irish exchequer. Only two original rolls survive, but a calendar prepared by the record commission covers the period 1294-1509. This calendar, often inaccurate and incomplete, consists of forty-three large manuscript volumes. In this study of Irish trade, which is largely confined to printed sources, a sample was taken from the memoranda rolls using nineteenth-century transcripts made by J. F. Ferguson. These transcripts were made from the original rolls and are very miscellaneous in character. They are often accompanied by an English translation. Some of Ferguson's extracts and transcripts are in the Public Record Office of Ireland and some in the library of the Royal Irish Academy. The information contained in the memoranda rolls is often of a detailed nature and similar to entries in the 'Catalogue of pipe rolls of the Irish exchequer' in *P.R.I. rep. D.K. 35-54,* which was in progress until the destruction of the Record Office in 1922.

Medieval material relating to Ireland in the Public Record Office, London, has been used extensively in the works of J. F. Lydon and G. O. Sayles. Recent publications by Robin Frame, T. E. McNeill and Kevin Down in particular refer to documents in the P.R.O. of particular interest to the social and economic history of medieval Ireland.

The Calendar of documents relating to Ireland and the Calendar of justiciary rolls of Ireland provide records of importance, but because they terminate in 1307 and 1314 respectively they are more illustrative of thirteenth-century conditions. Another great body of material has been gathered in the Calendar of the Carew manuscripts and state papers, which contain some late medieval material but mostly sixteenth-century documentation outside the scope of this study. The other major sources that span the entire period 1300-1500 are the Irish and Anglo-Irish annals, but these provide very little relating to trade. In his unrivalled studies of Gaelic Irish society in the later middle ages Kenneth Nicholls provides new insights into politics and points to the economic interdependence of the Irish and the Anglo-Irish.

A variety of source material dealing with particular towns, institutions and families served to add more detail to the framework built up from the records of central administration. The *Calendar of ancient records of Dublin,* the municipal records of Waterford and Galway edited by J. T. Gilbert in *H.M.C. rep. 10 Appendix V (1885),* the appendix of documents in James Hardiman's edition of Roderick O'Flaherty's *West Connaught,* and the *Blake Family records 1300-1599* are most useful. When these are examined together with Maurice Lenihan's *History of Limerick* and the records of the Arthur family of Limerick, a good indication of the internal trade of Dublin, Waterford, Galway and Limerick is given. It also becomes clear that a small merchant oligarchy controlled civic affairs in these towns. The *Calendar of Ormond Deeds,* the *Account roll of the Holy Trinity priory, Dublin,* the *Register of the wills and inventories of the diocese of Dublin 1457-1483* and the *Registers of the Archbishops of Armagh* indirectly yielded important details. English sources of a similar nature which proved useful include the publications of the Hakluyt Society and municipal records published by the record societies of Bristol and Southampton.

The standard texts on medieval Irish history devote little space to trade. A number of important articles published early in this century represent the beginnings of interest in medieval Irish commerce. W. F. T. Butler's 'Town life in medieval Ireland', T. J. Westropp's 'Early Italian maps of Ireland from 1300 to 1600 with notes on foreign settlers and trade' and Herbert Wood's 'Commercial intercourse with Ireland in the middle ages' are most useful. A. S. Green, *The making of Ireland and its undoing, 1200-1600*, contains much of interest but its value is impaired by lack of reference to sources and by frequent failure to distinguish between fourteenth- and sixteenth-century material.

M. D. O'Sullivan, *Italian merchant bankers in Ireland in the thirteenth century* provides a good commentary on the economic life of that century. Her *Old Galway* and William O'Sullivan's *Economic history of Cork city from the earliest times to the Act of Union* note many of the medieval trading references to both towns contained in the printed sources. Gearóid Mac Niocaill's monumental work *Na Buirgéisí, xii-xv aois* is the most comprehensive study of town life in medieval Ireland. Details of the administration of the towns are discussed and there is a good chapter on trade. More detailed work on Cork city has been published by A. F. O'Brien, who has similar studies of medieval Youghal and Kinsale forthcoming. H. B. Clarke's book on medieval Dublin will have contributions by archaeologists and geographers as well as historians. The publications of the *Urban Archaeology Survey* under the direction of John Bradley and the *Irish Historic Towns Atlas* will provide the necessary topographical complement to the work of the historians.

The histories of various Irish and English ports are among the most valuable secondary studies for the history of Irish trade, in particular the works of Irish historians writing before 1922 such as P.H. Hore, *History of the town and county of Wexford,* James Hardiman, *History of the town and county of Galway* and John D'Alton, *History of Drogheda and its environs,* who used materials that have since been destroyed. In addition to Carus-Wilson's works on Bristol and Wilson's on Chester, Colin Platt's *Medieval Southampton* and a variety of works on Welsh economic history by E. A. Lewis are also useful, in particular his 'The development of industry and commerce in Wales during the middle ages'.

There are some brief references in the works of French economic historians to trade with Ireland in the later middle ages. Michel Mollat's *Le commerce maritime normand à la fin du moyen âge* and Jacques Bernard's 'The Maritime intercourse between Bordeaux and Ireland *c.* 1450- *c.* 1520' are studies that indicate that more detailed work on medieval Irish trade will have to make use of the records of the continental ports.

Apart from A. E. J. Went's articles on aspects of Irish fisheries, which appeared in a variety of journals, there are few references to specific areas of medieval Irish trade, although a number of monographs on England's medieval trade are relevant to Ireland. In particular M. K. James's *Studies in the medieval wine trade* and E. M. Veale's *The English fur trade in the later middle ages* are of considerable importance and some contributions in *English trade in the fifteenth century*, edited by Eileen Power and M. M. Postan, refer to Anglo-Irish trade in the later middle ages.

English merchant shipping 1460-1540 by Dorothy Burwash assembles material illustrative of ships and shipping that frequented the Irish ports and a comprehensive European view is provided by R. W. Unger's technical study *The ship in the medieval economy, 600-1600*. No book touching the history of seafaring in Ireland could fail to acknowledge the work of John de Courcy Ireland, whose numerous books and articles have served to stimulate interest and research in all aspects of Irish maritime history.

In the following pages the activities of merchants in fourteenth- and fifteenth-century Ireland are arranged according to trading commodities, while a separate chapter deals specifically with ships and maritime affairs. The nature of the sources on which this study is based makes it virtually impossible to quantify the country's imports and exports or to illustrate trends by means of meaningful graphs and diagrams, although future researchers may exploit records capable of such analysis. In the meantime this book is an attempt to present the life and work of 'ordinary' people, namely, townsfolk and sailors — the merchants and mariners of medieval Ireland.

I

Food and Drink

In the middle ages large quantities of corn were grown in Ireland, where the Anglo-Norman settlers had established manorial farming. The principal areas were the well-drained lands of Leinster and east Munster and particularly counties Dublin, Louth, Meath and parts of Westmeath. In the knowledge that wheat cannot be cultivated on the same land for two years running, without serious harmful effects, a two- and a three-course crop rotation was practised on the manors. Yields were low. On the best farms a return of five times the amount sown was the average for wheat, with barley yielding perhaps half as much again but oats slightly less than wheat.[1] Some indication of the amount of corn grown on these farms can be seen in the huge consignments which were requisitioned as supplies for the Scottish wars of Edward I. The mid-fourteenth century saw a decline in the acreage under corn, due principally to the increasingly disturbed state of the country. Farming in the marcher or border areas returned to a more pastoral type, since the cow was less affected by the vagaries of war and weather.

In England also, at the beginning of the fourteenth century, the seeds of decline became evident after the economic expansion of the twelfth and thirteenth centuries. Population began to stabilize or fall; villages and arable land dropped out of use. This social and economic change was advanced by a series of bad harvests in the early decades of the century and reached a climax in 1348 with the advent of the Black Death, when an estimated one-third of Europeans died.[2]

In Ireland the drift away from large-scale tillage of the manorial type was particularly noticeable in Tipperary and Kilkenny. The problem increased in the early fifteenth century with many labourers emigrating to England, as a result of which Parliament declared in 1409-10, that 'the husbandry and tillage of the land is on the point of being altogether destroyed and wasted'. There is no evidence of a decline in corn growing in the Dublin-Meath-Louth area, which was producing more than enough for the needs of its towns and was sending grain to the southern ports of Wexford, Waterford, Ross, Youghal and Cork, as well as to Ulster, Wales and England in the later fourteenth and early fifteenth centuries.[3]

There are about two hundred references to the export of corn from Irish ports in the patent and close rolls between 1300 and 1450. Almost all are permits and licences to ship wheat, oats or barley out of the country. When these are looked at along with the orders requisitioning military supplies, some notion can be formed of the nature of the corn trade in medieval Ireland. There is difficulty, however, in establishing the role of the merchants in this trade and of determining how much corn was exported on a commercial basis. This can be seen when the licences and orders are divided into categories.

Firstly, licences were issued to magnates and religious houses in England, either to buy corn in Ireland or to ship the produce of their Irish farms to supply the needs of their households. Secondly, orders were given to requisition and export grain for the sustenance of the townspeople and occupants of castles in north Wales, at Carlisle, and for the royal armies abroad. Thirdly, licences were issued to take grain to Scotland, Ulster and the southern Irish towns. Fourthly, permits were granted to export grain to England, Gascony, Spain and Portugal, 'to make profit' or to sell in exchange for other goods.

Certain abbeys in the north-west of England frequently took corn from Ireland. The Abbey of Holm Cultram, perhaps because of its location in the marches, sent men and ships to buy corn in Ireland at least eight times between 1302 and 1323. The Premonstratensian canons of Cockersand, in Lancashire, were permitted to buy corn in 1382 'as the abbey is situate in great peril on the sea shore'.[4] Furness Abbey, also in Lancashire, appears regularly on the list of permits granted between 1315 and 1402 as a purchaser and purveyor of grain in Ireland. The Cistercians of this abbey had a number of manors and granges in Ireland, notably Beybeg near Drogheda, and owned several properties in that town. The abbey of Llanthony near Gloucester, held extensive lands in Meath and great amounts of food and fish were exported to England by the clerical proctors acting for the mother house. The prebend of Swords (Co. Dublin) is another ecclesiastical holding frequently held by English clerics in medieval times that is mentioned in connection with grain exports.[5]

Sometimes dignitaries such as the earl of Lancaster found it convenient to ship corn from Ireland for their own needs. Walter de Istelep sent men to Ireland in 1321 for corn, which was carried over in the *Katerine* of Dublin. Some absentee lords such as the earl of Norfolk found it more profitable to grow corn for sale in Ireland. Kevin Down has shown that the proceeds from the sale of corn on some of the earl's Co. Wexford manors in the 1280s were greater than the total of all the other income from his farms. Others who owned manors in Ireland were accustomed to have the fruits of the harvest conveyed to England when necessary. Licences were sometimes needed to do this and were granted at various times to Thomas Wogan, Edmund Lorence (the escheator of the county of Lancaster), and Robert Holywod. The transfer of victuals by those who owned lands both in Ireland and England to and from these countries was made easier as a result of legislation passed in 1361.[6]

The second series of permits consists of those which are linked to the politics of the English realm in the later middle ages. At the end of the thirteenth and the beginning of the fourteenth centuries, the king's chief concerns were with Scotland and France, and Ireland's main contribution was in food supplies. Ireland proved herself one of the king's greatest storehouses of grain, if not the main one according to Professor Lydon. In 1298, for example, she contributed 8,000 quarters* of wheat, 10,000 quarters of oats, 2,000 quarters of malt, along with beef, pigs, wine and fish. This amount of grain would have required upwards of 30,000 statute acres in tillage. In the final phase of the war, 1322-5, over 10,000 quarters of grain were purveyed and sent from Co. Meath.[7]

Such purveyances affected normal trading, and the practice of arresting corn at markets annoyed merchants. There were disturbances in Dublin in 1304, sparked off by royal purveyors procuring supplies for Scotland. Boroughs and market towns objected to this violation of their privileges in 1322. The clergy also were annoyed and threatened with excommunication anyone who arrested their corn. With the ending of the Anglo-Scottish war, large-scale requisitioning of food supplies on the king's behalf ceased.[8]

Grain supplies were collected and sent also to Gascony and Aquitaine. In the late thirteenth century large shipments were sent from Waterford and Ross. In 1324 5,000 quarters of wheat and 1,000 quarters of beans were sent to Aquitaine, and in 1344 the treasurer was ordered to buy 2,000 quarters of wheat in Ireland and ship it

---

*The quarter or in Ireland the *crannock* varied but generally averaged 8-10 bushels. The *wey* or *load* equalled five or six quarters.

to Bordeaux 'for the maintenance of the king's lieges there'. Gascony was always in need of corn from abroad, since so much of its farmland was given over to viticulture. Generally this corn was brought to Gascony by traders who were returning home with wine. Although considerable profits were made by some merchants — wheat bought in Ireland for 5s. a crannock was sold in Gascony for 22s. a crannock in 1305-7 — royal intervention was needed occasionally during the Hundred Years' War to supply the colony.[9]

'After Edward I's conquest of Wales, the erection of castles and the foundation of new boroughs gave impetus to trade, but a trade which was dictated by political more than economic considerations. Only in Beaumaris and to a lesser extent in Conway and Caernarvon did a merchant class emerge'. The evidence of the grain export permits would substantiate this, for in nearly every case concerning supplies sent from Ireland the town and the castle are linked. In 1316 Robert de Lughteburgh, a burgess of Aberconway, came to buy corn for the king's towns and castles of Caernarvon, Conway and Beaumaris. That same year the men of Caernarvon were permitted to buy corn in Ireland and Anglesey. There are further records of shipments in 1322-3, 1331, 1375, 1376 and 1422. It seems that most of the trade of north Wales was the monopoly of Chester merchants and frequently it was they who exported victuals from Ireland. Although Irish merchants made periodic calls with fish and corn, ordinary trade between north Welsh ports and Ireland was minimal.[10] The town and castle of Carlisle were in a similar situation to those in north Wales. Located on the Scottish marches, Carlisle's own harvests were often destroyed, but the town's proximity to the coast enabled it to receive shipments of victuals from Ireland. In 1307-8 the prior of St. Mary's in the town, as well as the bishop, received licences to import Irish corn. Andrew de Hartela, the earl of Carlisle, sent men and ships to Ireland for corn in 1322, and further supplies came in 1343 and 1356. Henry Percy, the earl of Northumberland, assumed the wardenship of Carlisle in 1402 and part of an agreement between himself and the king allowed him to buy 500 quarters of wheat annually in Ireland.[11]

The group of permits that concerns exports to Scotland, Ulster and the southern Irish towns can also be linked with political developments. With the ending of the Anglo-Scottish war in 1327 there was a short period during which frequent consignments of Irish grain went to Scotland. With the renewal of hostilities trade was affected by blockades enforced by the English king, but Scotland's need of corn meant that merchants often evaded the ban and traded

23

with the Scots. Among the accusations brought against one James Cotenham during the reign of Richard II was that he thrice sent ships to Scotland with wine, flour and other merchandise contrary to statute, and brought false money from Scotland to Ireland. The sale of corn to Scotland may partly explain the very high proportion of Scottish coins found in Irish hoards, particularly in Ulster and dating from the period 1351-1460. Truces made during the war coincide with permits issued for the legal shipment of corn to Scotland.[12]

The perilous position of the declining colony in eastern Ulster increased its dependence on supplies arriving by sea from the farmlands of Louth, Meath and Dublin. Sometimes we are told that the corn was destined for the castles of Carrickfergus or Carlingford but, as in the north Welsh castles and boroughs, it is likely that the townspeople shared the victuals. The *Godok* of Carrickfergus carried wheat, oats and stone-coal to the town *c*. 1320. In 1375 the mayor of Carrickfergus was licensed to import eight weys of wheat and John Wyk, a merchant of the town, a quantity of malt and oats. In the following year another leading public figure in the town, James Boys, the parson of the church, got a two-year licence to bring sixty weys of wheat, oats and other corn from Dublin to Drogheda. Corn supplies for Carrickfergus, Carlingford and Greencastle generally came from the Drogheda area. Merchants such as Thomas Rath of Drogheda sometimes brought corn and sold it, presumably at a large profit, to the beleaguered inhabitants. The plight of the Ulster ports was sometimes similar to that of Bordeaux and occasionally government intervention was needed to ensure supplies.[13]

The town of Carrickfergus, although effectively cut off by land, functioned as a trading port in the shelter of its strong castle. Merchants and ships of the town are occasionally noted in English and Irish ports. In common with many other towns in the later middle ages, Carrickfergus had probably worked out a *modus vivendi* with the local Irish. In the event of any attacks by enemies, tax reliefs were immediately sought and usually granted by the king.[14]

At times in the later fourteenth and early fifteenth century many of the southern Irish ports had difficulty in maintaining supplies of what Fernand Braudel called 'the trinity of grain, flour and bread ... the major preoccupation of towns, states, merchants and ordinary people for whom life meant "eating one's daily bread"'. A decline in the number of tenants on manorial farms in the south, increasing disorder among cadet branches of the Desmonds and Butlers, and the resurgence of Gaelic families combined with poor harvests to produce frequent corn shortages in the hinterlands of most of the

1 *Carrickfergus*, a sixteenth century drawing (British Library, Cotton
Ms Augustus I, ii, 42) The strong thirteenth century castle and
the number of late medieval tower houses give the little town an
embattled appearance. Essential supplies frequently arrived by sea
and ships of Carrickfergus are often mentioned in medieval trading
records.

ports, although those of Co. Cork appear to have been worst affected. In 1375 Wexford, Ross, Waterford, Youghal and Cork all received corn from the Meath-Dublin area. The permits for this particular year give a good indication of the great variety of people who received permits to trade and make money in corn in later medieval Ireland. Among these were: Walter Pierce and Richard Hassan, both from Wexford, who shipped corn to that town; Sir Robert de la Froigne, who brought some to Ross; and the earl of Desmond, who supplied a quantity to Waterford. Two merchants of Youghal brought a shipload to their own town and the bishop of Meath got a permit to ship wheat and malt to Cork.[15]

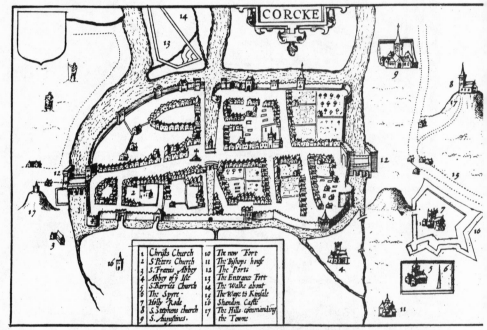

2 *Cork, c.* 1600 (John Speed, *The theatre of the empire of Great Britain,* London, 1611) Stanihurst remarked in 1577 that the people of Cork 'trust not the country adjoining but match in wedlock among themselves only, so that the whole city is well nigh linked one to the other in affinity'.

Cork, Youghal and Kinsale are grouped together in a number of permits issued in 1386-7, and in 1389-90 a general licence was issued to the men of Cork to purchase grain in any port for the support of the town. The difficulties of these three towns must have been considerable, for in 1393 they were forced to get grain supplies overland from Co. Limerick. This would have greatly increased the cost of the wheat, to which were added the customs and fees demanded by the earl of Desmond in return for protection. Corn continued to come by sea to the Co. Cork towns, mainly from the Dublin-Meath area, throughout the later fourteenth and early fifteenth centuries.

From legislation passed in 1449 it would appear that, although the southern ports lacked corn, they were not otherwise too disadvantaged. Contemporary merchants of these towns were bringing to Dublin and Drogheda wine, salt, iron and fish which they sold in exchange for corn, and this appears to have been a regular trading pattern throughout the fifteenth century.[16]

In earlier sections of this chapter shipments of Irish corn for domestic and military uses have been noted. But it is not clear how far this activity was connected with ordinary trade. As regards the war supplies, merchant shipping was used to transport the victuals and, in the case of grain shipments to the southern towns, what began to the accompaniment of pleas and cries for aid soon developed into a regular pattern of trade. Upwards of forty licences to send corn to England on a commercial basis were issued between 1320 and 1422. The general impression is not that there was a regular and specific export trade in Irish corn, but that merchants often included amounts of corn in their ships going to England and occasionally, in years of plenty, carried full cargoes across. Prominent merchants such as John Malpas of Waterford, William Symcock of Drogheda and Richard Taillour of Swords, who traded in wine, fish and hides with England, Scotland, France and Spain, are mentioned as exporters of corn and English merchants returning home were sometimes licenced to take corn with them.[17]

A number of licences for 1352 can be taken as typical. In that year the mayor and bailiffs of Dublin, 'impoverished by the late pestilence and other misfortunes', were licensed to buy 1,000 quarters of wheat in Ireland to sell in England. Robert Goldewell of Buckingham, merchant, was permitted to buy 300 quarters of wheat and oats in Ireland and 'make his profit' with them in England. William Folyn, Robert Somenour and Roger Wodehull were each licensed that year to buy 200 quarters of wheat and sell them in England, Wales or Gascony.[18]

Chester, perhaps owing to its position across the sea from the main corn-producing area in Ireland, received consignments occasionally, a trade that was established by the end of the eleventh century, according to William of Malmesbury. Licences to export

corn to England are rare after 1422. This may be due in part to changed legislation, but more probably to the plentiful and reliable grain supplies coming to England from central Poland and Prussia in the fifteenth century.[19]

Irish corn went to Gascony as part of the general commerce connected with the medieval wine trade. Irish merchants such as Nicholas Finglas of Dublin, when sailing to Gascony for wine, would sometimes include corn in the cargo. Gascon shipmasters, among them Myngod de Troy and Mamonyn de Manos, brought Irish corn on the return journey to Bayonne. The ubiquitous Bristol men were shipping Irish corn to Gascony, most probably in connection with the wine trade, and merchants going further afield to Spain and Portugal for wine found in these countries a market for Irish corn.[20]

Legislation was passed frequently to control corn exports. The main reasons were to maintain home supplies, to keep down prices, and to ensure that corn was not sent to the king's enemies. The sheriffs and specially appointed searchers were to enforce the laws in the ports. In 1355 there was a ban on exports from Ireland and special licences were required to take any corn out of the ports. Ships laden with corn in Drogheda were put under arrest.[21] A ban was always imposed on exports when an expedition was coming to Ireland. This happened in 1361 when Lionel, the duke of Clarence, was expected; in 1368 when William of Windsor was coming; in 1394 and 1398 when the king himself was due; and in 1424 in preparation for the arrival of Edmund Mortimer. A number of Bristol merchants complained in 1397 that the ban on exports of corn from Ireland, while the king was there with his army, had affected their trade. They were granted a licence to buy victuals in Ireland despite the ban.[22]

Special licences were required during such prohibitions and the laws were apparently enforced with some thoroughness. The searchers were not idle, since a number of arrests were made in 1399-1400 for amounts of less than twenty quarters. The memoranda rolls of the exchequer contain many such details of arrests, as well as information on corn prices. The case of Robert Eustace, who was illegally exporting corn in 1472, indicates that the corn laws were generally taken seriously. Robert had a consignment of corn in store, but it took heat and no one would buy it. He could not find anyone who was willing to hire a boat for taking the grain to Wales, as boat-owners were afraid of the consequences. So he himself bought a 'pickard', or small sailing boat, and was transporting the corn to Wales when he was caught.[23]

When the export of corn was banned in 1472, the home supplies were apparently running short and any grain produced was needed in England. Earlier there are few references to corn imported from England, except in times of famine. Before the coming of the Anglo-Normans there may have been some import trade in corn from England, since Giraldus mentions in his account of the attack on Wexford in 1169 that a merchant ship, lately arrived from Britain with corn and wine, was cut adrift in the harbour. With the establishment of the colony in the late twelfth and early thirteenth centuries, more land came under the plough and extensive tillage farming was well established by the fourteenth century.

Despite the harsh years 1315-7, when bad harvests and Edward Bruce's 'scorched earth' policy combined to cause a severe shortage, production recovered quickly, especially in the east midlands, and ample grain was produced here for home needs and for export. Over 5,000 quarters of grain were purveyed for the king in 1324. There was one bad period from 1328 to 1333 when severe weather led to a shortage of corn. The annals, both Irish and Anglo-Irish, have entries relating to this. Friar Clyn of Kilkenny refers to the cost of corn as being more than one mark a quarter in the winter of 1330-1 and he implies that imported corn kept prices high.[24] The imported corn came chiefly from south-western England, and among the earliest to receive supplies were the justiciar and the royal castles. Corn came from Gloucestershire and Somerset and English merchants from Gloucester, Bristol, Worcester and Salisbury brought consignments. Merchants from Cork — Stephen Travers, Henry Skidy, Augustine Gaynor and others — were licensed to bring corn from Bristol in the early 1330s.[25]

Shortly after this scarcity the decline in production in the south of Ireland set in, which led the southern towns to get their grain supplies from the Dublin-Meath area. Limerick city was importing corn in the fifteenth century, despite the fact that the county had relieved the Cork ports in 1393. A Breton merchant, Maurice de la Noe, was issued with a three-year licence in 1449-50 to victual Limerick with corn, honey, salt and other merchandise 'as he used to'. Some foodstuffs, including corn, began to be imported from the Bristol area again in the later fifteenth century. The amounts as shown in the customs accounts were not large. Beans were the main item, averaging in the region of 1,500 to 2,000 quarters in certain years.[26]

Herring fisheries The herring was a vital element in the prosperity of the maritime peoples of northern Europe; from Sligo to Riga medieval fishermen lived by the herring. In the fourteenth and fifteenth centuries there were two great herring fishing areas: the Western Baltic, which was controlled by the Hanseatic League, and off the east coast of England which was fished by the English and the Dutch. About 1450 the migrating herring from the Baltic appeared in increasing numbers in the North Sea, the Irish Sea and off the southern and western coasts of Ireland. This migration of herring shoals, which contributed in no small way to the decline of the Hanseatic League, in turn led to increased prosperity in Ireland, particularly in the south-west and west. It was realised that the shoals could move away again at any time and the transient nature of herring fisheries was recognised in a statute passed in 1470: '... herring fishing is always casual and movable by storms and winds from one place to another ... if the herrings are not taken at once they will be gone'.[1]

Another very important factor concerning herring fishing then as now, was that freshly caught herrings lost their flavour quickly and had to be treated within twenty-four hours. Unlike cod, it is difficult to sun-dry fatty fish like the herring, so in order to preserve them they have to be salted or smoked. Coinciding with the boom in herring fishing in the North Sea and off the Irish coast, and perhaps not unconnected with it, came a new way of storing herring. This method developed by the Dutch in the late fourteenth century meant that as soon as the fish were caught they were gutted, salted and packed in barrels head to tail in layers, each layer separated by salt. The barrels were then tightly sealed.

Salted herrings, on which noble households, merchants, monasteries and armies all relied heavily, were among the chief sources of preserved food in medieval Europe. A wealthy, well-organised fifteenth century English household such as the Paston family, whose account books and letters survive, expected to buy half a last, amounting to 6,000 North Sea herrings for £2 in the autumn, when supplies were plentiful and the wise housewife stocked up for Lent. During that penitential season the recommended breakfast for a young nobleman, in this case Lord Percy, aged eleven, was three white herrings or a dish of sprats, a piece of salt fish, bread, butter and beer![2]

There appear to have been two clear divisions in the medieval Irish herring trade: the fisheries of the Irish Sea, which were closely bound up with the ports of Dublin and north Leinster, and the herring fisheries off the south-western and western coasts, which benefitted local Irish and Anglo-Irish families.

Herring fishing in the Irish Sea Herrings were plentiful in the Irish Sea throughout the fourteenth and fifteenth centuries and there are frequent references to boats fishing for them. Scottish fishing boats from Rutherglen, near Glasgow, were trading herrings in Dublin and Drogheda in 1306 and in 1337 the abbot of Inch Abbey (Co. Down) had a court at Munkhill 'near the shore, in Tevere tenement for herring fishers in the season'. Herring boats were taxed for the use of Bullock Harbour (near Dalkey) in 1345-6 and for calling at Kilclogher (probably Clogherhead, Co. Louth) in 1475-7. The evidence from the Chester customs accounts indicates the importance of the herring fisheries of the Irish Sea. The published customs accounts show large consignments of herring being shipped from Drogheda and the ports of Co. Dublin. In fact Ireland's chief export to Chester until the mid-fifteenth century was herring and it is not surprising to note that Chester's main export to Ireland at this time was salt.[3]

Evidence from other sources suggests that the trade in herrings was concentrated in the ports of Dublin, Drogheda, Malahide, Howth and Rush. It would appear also that the trade was managed by fish merchants who brought the catches of the fishing fleets (not always herrings) in these ports for re-sale in the towns or for export. In 1385 Walter Taillour of Swords was licenced to buy fish in Co. Dublin and take them to Chester and Liverpool, while in 1403 John Slene of Rush was permitted to export 4,000 salted fish to England.[4]

The Pale area, with its concentration of towns, would have used large quantities of fish. The supplies for Dublin would have come from the numerous small ports and landing places from Skerries southwards. Sometimes only small quantities arrived for sale at the fish market in Fishamble Street and when this happened the selling prices were often double or treble the official price set by law. A statute of 1355 explains that shortages and high prices were the result of private merchants and others forestalling the market. Forestallers bought the fish directly from the fishermen, carted them away to be processed and then exported the cured product secretly avoiding all taxes and tolls due to the municipality or the government. Having commandeered most of the catch landed on a particular day, the forestallers could get the highest prices for whatever amount of fish they decided to sell in the city. The citizens, rich and poor, noble and clerical, had to pay up because they needed fish to eat on fast days and days of abstinence. These were not just a matter of personal piety but were imposed by statute, and all over Latin Christendom municipal regulations forbade the sale of meat on Fridays. Officials were ordered to search out the forestallers; to go looking for them two and three times a week if necessary. When any were found, they were to be confined in Dublin Castle, there to await exemplary punishment while their fish were confiscated for official consumption. There are records of some small time operators who were caught, like John Englond of Corduff a worker in the harbour of Rush in 1400 who was accused of illegally selling six dozen cod, ling and conger in Malahide. But his few fish cannot have made much difference to the market.[5]

A contract to supply a noble household must have been keenly sought after, but it was not without its drawbacks. The seneschal of Wexford, who undertook to supply the earl of Ormond with victuals and fish while he was in Wexford for Christmas 1393, did so, risking a fine of £100 if supplies failed. Two Co. Dublin merchants John Greyn of Malahide and William Veer of Howth contracted to supply the justiciar's household with fish as it travelled on circuit around Ireland in 1383. For Richard II's expedition to Ireland in 1394, however, officials were not prepared to take any chances with supplies from Irish fishermen but ordered the arrest in England of 'as many fishermen with the vessels, boats, nets, instruments and other engines as will suffice for catching fish at sea for the use of the household during the present expedition to Ireland'.[6]

The herring remained plentiful in the Irish Sea during the sixteenth century. The fisheries around Ardglass were particularly valuable and the income from the customs of these fisheries went to the earl of Kildare in 1515. Exports continued and obviously were blamed for shortages in the home market. Henry VIII in proposing legislation to the earl as chief governor in 1515, noted 'that whereas merchants convey out of this land into France, Brittaine and other strange parts, salmonds, herrings, dry lings, haaks and other fish, so abundantly that they leve none within the land to vitall the King's subjects here in so much that uneth (i.e scarcely) any such fish may be had for mony'. An idea of the scale of the fishing can be seen in the fact that an English fishing fleet of 600 boats was operating around Carlingford in 1535 and the fishermen offered to make 3,000 fighting men available for two or three days to help the lord treasurer and his forces who were campaigning in the area.[7]

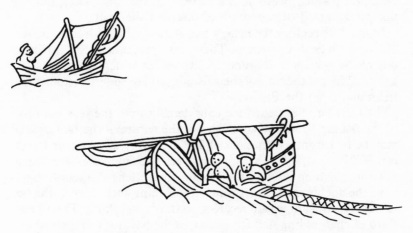

3   *Fishing in the Irish Sea,* c. 1580 (*Facs. nat. Mss Ire.,* IV, 1) Drawings of fishery vessels from a map of north-east Ireland, from Dublin to Carrickfergus.

Herring fishing off the Atlantic coast The extent of the herring fisheries off the south-western and western coasts was no less sizeable, but it was of a different nature. In this region English and foreign fishermen, having caught herring and other fish offshore, used the bays and havens as anchorages where they could process the catch.

For the right to shelter and use the fishing grounds in safety, the fishermen paid certain dues to the local magnates, whether Irish chieftains or Anglo-Irish lords. These payments annoyed the government and steps were taken in 1465 to prevent foreign vessels from fishing 'among the King's Irish enemies' without special licence. Significantly boats fishing in the Irish Sea north of Wicklow were exempted, since their catches would have been landed in the ports of the Pale area to the benefit of the King's lieges. The statute declared that the Irish were being 'much advanced and strengthened as well in victuals and harness as divers other necessaries, also great tributes of money given by every of the said vessels'. This was not the first enactment of this nature, for in 1449-50 parliament tried to prevent commercial fishing off Baltimore in west Cork because of the profit in victuals and arms it brought to Fineen O'Driscoll. The date of the latter decree, which was directed against fishermen from Wexford, Waterford, Youghal, Cork and Kinsale, coincides with the time when the herring shoals were on the increase in the south-west, but had not yet attracted the attention of foreign fishermen.

In the next century the fishery was at its height, with fleets of over 600 Spanish boats in the area. There was a proposal in 1572 to fortify one of the islands in Baltimore Harbour 'in which the Spanish lie aground during the time of their fishing' and to collect customs from them and from the Biscayans.[8]

The local families benefitted considerably from the seasonal visits of the fishing fleets and some idea of the nature of the fees exacted may be had from a document of 1482. In May of that year James, earl of Desmond, settled a dispute between two families named Treunt regarding fishing dues in the Dingle area. Richard Treunt was to have the anchorage charges imposed on ships anchoring in the bay of Ventry. Richard was to receive two-thirds and Philip Treunt one-third of charges imposed for fishing in the bay, for using the shore, for salting fish, or for drying the nets. Both were to share other duties accruing from fishing and netting within the bay. Early sixteenth-century records refer to Spaniards paying £300 a year to Mac Fineen Duff of Ardee, a local chief, for liberty to fish in Kenmare Bay. The head of this sept had several deeds signed and sealed by his ancestors in connection with this fishery. Charles Smith in his history of Cork (1750), mentions Kinsale fishermen coming to Cape Clear, where they built huts to cure their fish and for which they paid 'a smart rent'.[9]

The Irish families themselves do not appear to have involved themselves in these sea fisheries but seemed content with the income from the levies, which sometimes included certain tithes of fish. A sixteenth century source mentions that at one time Biscayans and Spaniards rendered to the local chieftains the sixth and tenth fish of all they took between Baltimore and the Blaskets. They appeared to have kept a close eye on their rights and presumably rowed their galleys around where the fleets fished. They also provided protection for foreign boats fishing in their territories. O'Sullivan of Beare, whose lordship was in the Bantry Bay area, once captured and executed the captain of an English ship who had taken a Spanish boat fishing off Dursey Island.[10]

The herring fisheries of the north-western coast, which were of great value to O'Donnell of Donegal, did not fully develop until the sixteenth century. Around 1400 there was an important export trade

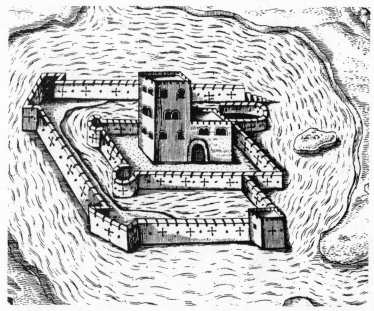

4 *Carrigafoyle Castle, Co. Kerry* (*Pacata Hibernia*, London, 1633) Built in fifteenth or early sixteenth century by O'Connor-Kerry this fine tower house with a fortified harbour is situated on an island in an inlet near the mouth of the Shannon. Nearby is the Friary of Lislaughtin founded for the Observantine Franciscans in 1470.

in salmon from this area, a good deal of which went to Bristol. In the fifteenth century the Bristol records show the import of large quantities of Irish herrings. In 1403-4 338 lasts (over 4 million) of herring worth almost £1,000 were imported and in 1479-80 370 lasts worth £1,233.

Heryng of Slegoye and salmon of Bame (Bann)
Heis made in Brystowe many a ryche man.

According to this fifteenth-century English proverb the herring came mainly from the Sligo area, yet it seems more likely that until the sixteenth century the fish came to Bristol from the south-western coast. In 1449 a Bristol boat, fishing off the Cork coast, captured a Spanish ship.

A Bristol merchant was sent to purchase herring in Kinsale in 1480 and in that year the custom account indicates that four of the ships bringing major consignments of herring to Bristol were vessels of the port of Cork.[11]

35

The herring fisheries brought greatly increased income to the south-west and west of Ireland in the later fifteenth century. This extra wealth is one explanation for the great renewal of building and refurbishing of monastic houses, friaries and castles that took place at this time, in particular in the Gaelic and gaelicised areas of the western seaboard.

5 *Ross Errilly, Co. Galway* (drawing by H.G. Leask, 1937) This Franciscan friary was founded in the mid-fourteenth century by Sir Raymond de Burgo. Most of the present building dates from the later fifteenth century, by which time the friars had adopted the strict Observantine code.

Cod, hake and other sea fisheries The later medieval sea fisheries of Ireland included cod, ling and hake as well as herring. Cod (also called milwell) was very plentiful in the cold waters of the north Atlantic, where most of the fishing was done by Norwegians. Almost all of the catch was sun-dried and exported as 'stockfish' or 'hard fish'. This dried cod appears to have been something of a rarity in fourteenth-century Ireland, for in 1329 Robert Bruce sent a present to the Red Earl of Ulster of 200 'hard fish'. In the fifteenth century the Icelandic cod fisheries developed and attracted many fishermen and merchants from England. Those from Bristol travelled to Iceland via the western coast of Ireland and in all likelihood contributed to the growth of the town and port of Galway. Irish fishermen do not appear to have shared in the Icelandic fisheries, although on one ill-fated venture in 1457 Drogheda merchants did join with some men of Chester on a trading voyage to Iceland.[12]

Quantities of cod and ling were caught off the Irish coast. The monks of Llanthony Abbey shipped cod and salmon to England occasionally, presumably for their own use. In the fourteenth century the bishop of Cloyne was supplied with ling, cod and haddock at special rates by his tenants at Ballycotton, Co. Cork, as part of their rent. A consignment of cod and ling valued at 52s. arrived at Poole, in Dorset, from Youghal, Co. Cork, in 1504.[13]

Hake was another sea fish that was caught in considerable quantities in fifteenth-century Ireland. It appears that the hake fisheries were concentrated off the southern coast between Waterford and Cork. The village of Ballyhack, on the shores of Waterford harbour, was one important fishing centre in the area. The Cistercians of nearby Dunbrody Abbey had tithes of all fish landed at Ballyhack and perhaps it was in connection with the fishery that the strong fifteenth- or early sixteenth-century tower-house, which dominates the quay in the little village, was erected. Large quantities of hake were exported. In 1504-5 Bristol imported from various ports in south-eastern Ireland 90,099 hake valued at £455 3s. 6d.[14]

Boats from the southern Welsh ports of Chepstow, Tenby, Milford and Carmarthen did much of the carrying trade between Bristol and Ireland. They took from Ireland herrings, hake, salmon, salted fish, hides and Irish cloth and returned with salt, iron, wine and English cloth.

Herring seem to have been the only important element in the Irish sea fish trade prior to 1400, but the sea fisheries developed quickly in the century that followed. In 1430 the king claimed to be losing 300-400 marks annually because of illegal exports of salted fish. It was primarily the migration of the herring shoals from the Baltic and their continual increase in the seas off the south-western and western coasts of Ireland throughout the century that made fish Ireland's most important product by the early sixteenth century.[15]

Freshwater and estuarine fish Salmon and eels were the principal types of fresh-water fish to figure in the trade of later medieval Ireland. Both these varieties were taken by the use of weirs: the eels in specially developed riverine weirs, the salmon in riverine and estuarine weirs. The majority of the fishing weirs of medieval Ireland were in the hands of the monasteries, chiefly as a result of grants made by their founders. A number of river fisheries were held by the king, notably the principal weirs on the Shannon at Limerick and Athlone. In law, the tidal reaches and fisheries of every navigable river belonged to the king by his prerogative. A considerable number of law cases involving fisheries are recorded. The case of the Erne fisheries in 1934 recalled many disputes of medieval times and even consulted Brehon law regarding fisheries.[16]

All great landowners owned fishing weirs. The earl of Ormond had several on the Suir and Nore and the earl of Desmond had a lucrative fishery as part of his manor of Killorglin, Co. Kerry. Important townsfolk had weirs also, such as the Lynchs of Galway who controlled two on the River Corrib. Most of the monasteries leased their weirs but part of the rental generally included a regular supply of fresh fish. St. Mary's Abbey, Dublin, for example farmed out its fishery in Lough Ennel, Co. Westmeath, for £4 13s. 4d. and 100 fresh eels. The royal weirs were a valuable source of revenue, eagerly sought for rental by merchants. The king's weir on the Shannon at Limerick was worth 100 marks a year in the thirteenth century and the Bann fishery netted him £60 per annum in the early sixteenth century.[17]

Salmon fishing Salmon was always considered to be among the finest of edible fish and suitable fare to be set before distinguished guests, particularly on days of abstinence. Considering that Latin Christendom had upwards of one hundred days each year on which meat was forbidden, salmon was in constant demand, particularly in wealthy households.

Irish salmon was exported to England in large quantities during the later middle ages and both Irish and English merchants shared in the trade. Two citizens of Waterford were licensed to ship eight casks of salmon from either Wexford or Waterford in 1388-9. In 1441 an inquisition was held in Bristol to establish whether Geoffrey Galvey of Kinsale or his son owned fifty pipes of salmon that had been brought from Ireland. (A pipe or butt was equal to half a tun and of salmon was reckoned as 60 gallons). Four Irish merchants were arrested in Southampton in 1446 for exporting twenty-four pipes of salmon and sixteen barrels of herring without licence.

Between 1400 and 1416 upwards of thirty licences were issued to Bristol men to sail to Ireland with merchandise, chiefly old wine, salt and cloth, and return home with salmon and Irish goods. The phrasing of the permits follows a similar formula and varies only in regard to the size of the ship and quantities of goods carried.[19] One example will show the nature of this aspect of the export trade in salmon.[20] In 1400 a licence was issued for Thomas Clerk, master of the *Trinity* of Bristol and for William Stevens, John Alinere, William Pytte and Thomas Knappe, merchants of Bristol, to cross with sixteen mariners to the castle of Conere (probably O'Connor) in the town of Sligo in Ireland. They had twenty tuns of old wine which 'on account of its age and weakness' could not be sold in England, six lasts of salt and five packs of cloth called 'western cloth'.* They were to sell the wine and the cloth to the king's lieges and buy salmon in Sligo. Then, having salted the salmon, they were to return to England, pay all customs and sell the fish.

The Irish destination of the ships is not usually given. Although Sligo is named only once, it seems probable that all these vessels from Bristol came to the west of Ireland to buy salmon. Bristol men had an interest in the salmon fisheries of western Ireland prior to 1400. The valuable salmon fishery of Galway, which was in the king's hands in 1386-7, was secured by Richard Panys of Bristol for two years at £10 per annum.[21] The old corrupt wine that was carried to Ireland and used probably for pickling fish would have found a ready sale in the west. Likewise the small quantities of cloth carried is suggestive of trade with lesser ports rather than of dealings with established merchants in the ports of the east and south.

Merchants from English ports other than Bristol were also engaged in this salmon trade. William Soper, a leading merchant of Southampton, who traded to the Mediterranean, sent a ship with salt and wine to Ireland in 1426 to be exchanged for salmon and hides. A London fishmonger, Walter Aylwyn appointed attorneys to look after his interests in Ireland in 1392 and 1398, and the merchants of London who were permitted to bring to Ireland in 1405 sixty tuns of old wine were probably connected with the salmon trade.[22] This pattern of trade continued into the sixteenth century, as an example from Padstow in Cornwall illustrates:

> Whereas the custom and usage of the county ... time out of mind hath been that four, five or six more or less of the inhabitants in the county ... rigge, vitale and set forth one or divers ship in voyage towards the coasts of Ireland there to be laded with fish and other merchandise and at the return of the same, the said fish to be divided

---

*a 'last' of salt = 2 tons or 4,000 lbs. A 'pack' as a measure of cloth = 10 whole cloths of 24 yds. each or 20 cloths of 12 yds. each in length.

among them that did victual and maintain the ship. About September 1533 [the writer] did victual 1/10 part of three ships in the haven of Padstow, called the *Jane*, the *Anthony* and the *Nicholas* with 28 bushels of salt ... 7 bushels of flour, 3 hoggesheads and 3 barrels of beer and 33 shillings sterling in ready money to the intent that the ships should voyage to Ireland and there lade with hake, mylioyn fishes, ling fishes and white herring and then return to Padstow, which was done on November 24th last ....[23]

The Bann was the famous salmon fishery on the northern coast and, before the decline of the Anglo-Irish colony in Ulster, Coleraine was an important settlement. The account roll of the ministers of Elizabeth de Burgh lists income derived from fishing permits and licences to operate boats in the area in 1353-4 and in 1358-9. In the later fourteenth and early fifteenth century much of the external trade of the area appears to have been in the hands of Drogheda and Dublin merchants. When the Bann fishery came into the king's hands in 1386-7 (at the same time as the Galway weirs) it was rented by Molyneux and Symcock, two Drogheda merchants. Permits similar to those issued to the above-mentioned Bristol merchants were given to Drogheda shippers in 1409, allowing them to fish and trade 'in the parts of Ban in Ulster'. One of these ships brought a consignment of salt and twelve 'dozens' of English cloth, presumably to exchange it for salmon. The earl of Kildare was granted the fishery in the late fifteenth century and as likely as not made it a source of revenue for himself. When it was leased out again in 1519 a merchant of Chester, Otwell Corbett, took it at the high annual rent of £60 Irish.[24]

Predictably, the records show that Bristol was the port through which most Irish salmon exports reached the English market. This trade was already established by the late fourteenth century. During the fifteenth century there was a huge growth in demand, which continued into the sixteenth century when this trade was worth hundreds of pounds annually.[25]

In contrast, Chester does not seem to have imported any significant quantities of Irish salmon in the fourteenth and fifteenth centuries. The printed customs accounts show large quantities of herring and other fish coming from the ports of the Pale area, but only once is salmon mentioned specifically. This remains the case in the sixteenth century when, despite the fact that it becomes more difficult to identify the ports of origin of ships that paid customs at Chester, salmon rarely appears in any account. The trade of Chester was mainly with the ports of the eastern coast and the fact that those did not export salmon suggests that fish taken in the weirs of the Boyne and Liffey supplied the markets of Dublin and Drogheda.[26] This is a further indication that the extensive trade in the export of salmon was located in the west and north of Ireland. When the herring became plentiful in the same areas, the local ruling families prospered and were in a position to endow religious houses, build bridges and improve their castles.

Eel fishing The eel figured predominently on the menus of medieval households. They were eaten in religious houses and by aristocrats. A list of purchases made in Kilkenny by the earl of Ormond about 1400 includes two lots of eels among other fish. The wealthy Italian merchant, Francesco Datini of Prato (died 1410), was very fond of eels. He ate them pickled in their own fat with strong spices and wine or in a pie with spices, olive oil and orange and lemon juice. Apparently they were popular fare also, as an annalist mentions that during the severe winter of 1338, when the Liffey was frozen over in Dublin the people played football on the ice and made a fire on it with timber and turf on which they roasted eels. (Oysters were popular fare, too, and regulations governing their sale in Dublin are extant. Some of the oysters sold in Limerick were fished at the mouth of the Shannon as oyster boats passing Scattery Island had to give 1,000 oysters a year to St. Senan's monastery there.)[27] Eels would have been a particularly important source of fresh food in the middle ages since they could be kept alive for long periods in suitable boxes provided with running water. The archbishop of Armagh must have had extensive storage facilities for the great number of eels that he received as part of his rents. From Kilree manor in the bishopric of Derry he received annually in the fifteenth century 40,000 medium eels and 60 large eels. As he resided on his manor at Termonfechin during most of the middle ages he more than likely sold the eels in nearby Drogheda — if they arrived safely from Derry. More eels, 635 of them, came twice yearly to him along with 6 fat pigs, 36 gallons of butter and 6 marks in lawful money as the rent of his lands, at Inishkeen, Co. Monaghan.[28] Eel weirs were almost as valuable as salmon weirs: in Galway in 1283 they were valued at £10 and £11 a year respectively. Galway and Athlone appear to have been great sources of eels. In 1293 Thomas de Pykering accounted for £4 16s. from the sale of 3,600 eels at Athlone. Fish merchants brought eels from Athlone to Dublin, according to an incident related in *MacFirbis's Annals*. In 1452 English

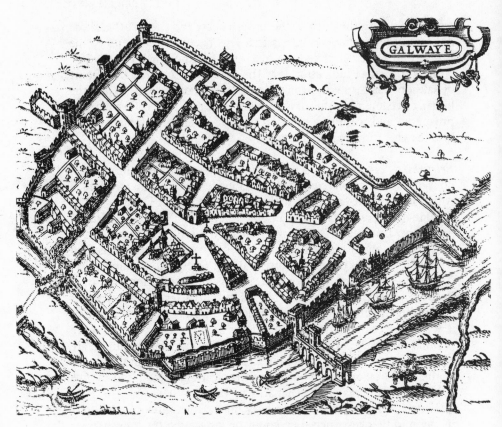

6 *Galway, c.* (John Speed, *The theatre of the empire of Great Britain*, London, 1611) Speed's drawing shows a well-defended substantial town. The importance of fisheries is evident from the small boats operating on the river and the man with the three-pronged fishing-spear heading for the country.

merchants, accompanied by Lysagh FitzRoss and some local Irish, were coming from Athlone via Athboy and Trim when they were attacked by Fearghal Óg MágEochagáin and the writer remarks that 'no man living shall give account of the multitude of eels that were lost'.[29]

Eels appear to have been sold for the home market and do not figure significantly in exports. Once only are they mentioned in the printed customs accounts of Bristol: this was in 1479-80 when thirty-four barrels of eels were included in a large cargo of goods from Ireland.

Fish undoubtedly formed an important part of the local trade between towns and their hinterlands in the middle ages. Fishing rights on rivers or estuaries near the ports were even more valuable, because of the proximity of the markets, and they were jealously guarded. Walter de Bermingham, lord of Athenry, complained in 1389-90 that certain Irishmen from Connacht were poaching in his waters. The king ordered the sheriff to put a stop to this and commanded the mayor of Galway to prevent the sale of the illegally caught salmon in the city.

In the Drogheda area a serious dipute over tithes of fish broke out between the procurators of Llanthony Priory and the local clergy. It was resolved by the archbishop of Armagh in 1430. In the valley of the Suir between Clonmel and Waterford, the earl of Ormond collected a yearly rent from fishermen operating boats on the river. Severe punishment was meted out to anyone who poached fish or withheld fishing tithes or dues. One Dublin fisherman, John Dyrre, who in 1425 operated from a boat belonging to St. Mary's Abbey, helped himself to two salmon due as tithes to the owners of that section of the Liffey fishery, the prior and community of Holy Trinity (Christ Church). By way of penalty he was ordered to be beaten by the curate around St. Michan's Church on six days, wearing nothing but a loincloth![30]

The wine trade with France From earliest times there was always a demand for wine in Ireland and, because the vine does not flourish here, all wine had to be imported. The ancient sagas and law tracts indicate that large quantities of wine were drunk by the noble classes and the necessity of wine for the celebration of Mass resulted in a heavy demand from the numerous monasteries. In the Life of St. Ciarán of Clonmacnoise, there is mention of wine from Gaul being brought up the Shannon to the monastery. In the twelfth century the Anglo-Norman historian, Giraldus Cambrensis, remarked that 'imported wines, conveyed in the ordinary commercial way, are so abundant that you would scarcely notice that the vine was neither cultivated nor gave its fruit there'.

At the end of the thirteenth century and the beginning of the fourteenth century the wine trade in Ireland, and the trade in foodstuffs, were dominated by the demand and supply of the wars of Edward I (1272-1307) in Wales and Scotland. Corn, meat and fish, the produce of this country, were purveyed by diligent collectors all over the east and south-east and made ready for transport from New Ross, Wexford, Waterford, Drogheda and Dublin. The wine, in common with almost all wine used in medieval Ireland and England, came from France, from the royal dependencies of Aquitaine and Gascony, to the same ports to be shipped along with the provisions.

It is important to note that, for medieval sailing ships, the ports of the east and south-east of Ireland were easier of access from south-western France than those of the west of England. Since substantial capital was required to finance these large shipments of wine and food, it is not surprising that Italian merchant-bankers played a major part in the enterprise.[1]

Because of the nature of surviving records, at home and abroad, it is impossible to quantify or draw up accurate tables of annual wine imports. The records of Bordeaux consist of wine customs accounts and notarial records, which are mainly fifteenth-century contracts for wine shipments. The wine customs indicate that Irish ships were active in carrying wine: in 1303-4 eighteen Irish ships carried out 1,648 tuns of wine and in 1307-8 the same number shipped 1,657 tuns. In these accounts the destination of the wine is unfortunately not given. Direct Irish participation in the trade was very small, since the annual turnover of the port at this time was almost 100,000 tuns.

With the decline of Bordeaux's exports, due to warfare and destruction, recorded Irish shipping dropped to one to five ships carrying 200-300 tuns annually. Only 22 of the 591 contracts surviving for the period 1455-99 specifically mention Irish destinations or merchants, and the amounts of wine are small — only 300 tuns in the busiest year, 1499.[2]

Both sets of records are incomplete and can serve chiefly to show some Irish participation in the trade of Bordeaux. In addition, Ireland received wine through La Rochelle and ports in Normandy and Brittany. Wine arrived in Irish and foreign ships, shipped sometimes by Irish, sometimes by English or alien merchants. The actual volume of wine imported will never be known, but a multitude of varied references indicate that the import trade in wine was a very important factor in the medieval Irish economy.

We cannot be sure how much extra wine was imported because of the king's demands for supplies. It is quite likely that a certain proportion of the normal imports was requisitioned for military use in particular years. For example, in December 1298 the king ordered 1,000 hogsheads* of wine for his expedition against the Scots, adding that 'if these were not found in Ireland the justiciar and treasurer were to treat with some merchants, in order to have them sent from Gascony'. In January 1300, 3,000 hogsheads were ordered from Ireland to be sent to Skinburness, a small port in south-western Scotland where the war supplies were landed. The documentation of these war supplies is relatively full, particularly towards the end of the reign of Edward I, and Ireland's contribution to his war effort has been expertly assessed by Professor James Lydon.[3]

During the reign of Edward I, merchants of Gascony and Aquitaine were active in the Irish wine trade. In 1288-9 the accounts of prise wines (see below p. 000) records the presence in Dublin of merchants from St. Milione, and in 1303, merchants of Bayonne were trading both in New Ross and in Dublin. The merchants of Bayonne kept a close eye on all aspects of Irish trade at this time, having been granted in 1299 the revenues of the customs on wools, hides and skins in Ireland, England and Scotland. They had these monies until 1304, when they handed over control of the customs to the Frescobaldi, Italian merchant-bankers.

The merchants of the port towns were also engaged in the wine trade at this time. William Joye, master of the *Patrick* of Youghal, and his associates shipped 117 tuns and one pipe of wine from

*Hogshead = 63 gallons; 2 hogsheads = 1 pipe; 2 pipes = 1 tun (252 gallons).

Lebourne in Gascony to Youghal in 1293-4. Wine came in non-Irish ships, such as the ship of Exmouth that brought 129 tuns to Cork in 1291-2 and the *Alice* of Harwich, which was in New Ross with 133 tuns of wine in 1292 and again with 180 tuns in 1299.[4]

The import of wine from Gascony to Ireland was part of a bilateral trade in which Irish products were taken out and marketed in Gascony and wines were purchased and shipped back. M.K. James, in her invaluable study of the medieval wine trade, noted that Irish hides and fish found a ready market in Bordeaux. She referred to tariffs of goods and services in the city archives as evidence that Bordeaux's need for hides must, very largely, have been met by the produce of Ireland.

There is an interesting early reference to Irish hides being carried to Gascony in exchange for wine. In 1307 the hearings for the canonisation of Thomas de Cantilupe at Hereford were interrupted by the arrival of a group of Irish sailors with a votive offering. They had been sailing from Ireland to a Gascon port for wine, with a cargo of hides and cloth, when on 3 October a storm arose and the boat was swamped. Not having a priest on board, the sailors all confessed their sins to one another and vowed (if they survived) to carry a ship of silver to the tomb of Thomas de Cantilupe at Hereford.

Gascony, with so much of its countryside given over to vineyards, was in constant need of corn and food supplies, and Irish corn was always in demand. In 1299 Arnald de Ambydones, a merchant, sued Walter de Mariseis, a mariner, for selling sixty crannocks* of his wheat at La Rochelle instead of Bayonne, as the price was better at Bayonne. A large number of the corn export permits recorded in the patent and close rolls in the fourteenth and fifteenth centuries refer to exports to Gascony. In 1404 Nicholas Woder of Dublin was licensed to bring six weys of wheat to Bordeaux in order to buy wine and in 1407-8 John Bussare exported twenty-eight weys to Bayonne. William Symcock, a Drogheda merchant whose name appears frequently, got a permit to ship eight weys of wheat to Gascony or Spain in 1386-7 and in the same year he was licensed to carry six tuns of wine to the islands off Scotland. In 1389-90 he was bringing wine (and beer) to London and to Ulster and in 1412 was again exporting wheat to Bordeaux.[5]

It is not clear from Irish and English sources how much fish was

*In medieval times weights and measures varied from one country to another and there can be much uncertainty about modern equivalents. Dry measures for grain etc. included 8 gallons = 1 bushel; 8 bushels = 1 quarter; 5 quarters = 1 wey; The crannock is uncertain, see above p. 22.

exported in exchange for wine. Gascony may well have had its fish supplied through the Hansa from the Baltic and North Sea. Wine was brought to Ireland in 1364 in exchange for English herrings. John de Neubourn was commissioned to buy forty lasts of herrings and ship them from Great Yarmouth to Bordeaux. With the money he was to buy 100 tuns of wine and bring it to Ireland for the household of the duke of Clarence, Edward II's third son and chief governor of Ireland. Around the beginning of the sixteenth century, when the herring became plentiful off the west coast of Ireland, a more direct exchange trade in fish and wine seems to have developed. A charter party agreement dated 3 July 1531 sent a ship to fish off Ireland. The master was to sail to Bordeaux with the first favourable wind after 10 September, sell the fish in the town and remain for three weeks after the wine had been made. The ship was then to sail to London with the wine. It was about this time also that O'Donnell got his title 'King of the fish' abroad. Perhaps it was in response to this that the Irish sometimes referred to the wine as the 'King of Spain's daughter'!

The wine trade was, like almost every aspect of medieval trade, based on an exchange of commodities. Sometimes Gascon or Spanish merchants arrived with wine and departed with Irish goods, sometimes Irish merchants sailed with hides or corn and came back with wine. Oftentimes, too, English merchants played an important part in the trade, either directly or through Irish agents. In 1319 Thomas Mustard, a burgess of Bristol, through his agent Walter atte Rode purchased fifteen great sacks of wool in Clonmel, intending to sell them in Bordeaux and to return with wine to Waterford. Walter, however, died suddenly in Bordeaux and, not having made a will, his goods and possessions were arrested by the authorities. Mustard got the mayor of Waterford to write to the seneschal of Gascony, explaining that Walter was his agent and that the confiscated goods were his property. The authorities in Bordeaux then held a sworn enquiry, during which two burgesses of Waterford in Bordeaux testified that they knew the deceased as Mustard's servant. One of them recounted that he had been in Clonmel when the wool was being weighed and had heard the instructions given to Walter as to its sale. Three Bristol merchants deposed to the same effect and added further details of the agreement between the merchant and his agent.

A similar case dragged on in the Irish courts for many years and concerned Olivia, wife of Thomas de Burgo, who in 1287 had sent to John le Engleys of Drogheda 115 tuns and seven pipes of wine from 'the parts of Bordeaux'. John died, having paid for only forty tuns. Olivia lost the documents of agreement owing to the war, and many merchants had to be called as witnesses.[6]

The wine trade with Spain and Portugal Most of the wine consumed in medieval Ireland came from France, but, linked no doubt to England's failing fortunes in Gascony, a trade in wine with Spain and Portugal began to develop towards the end of the fourteenth century. One of the early references to this trade is to a ship from Lisbon that was arrested in Waterford in 1374, because the mayor and bailiffs thought the master and sailors were 'the king's enemies'. Not long afterwards, in 1380, a proclamation was issued by the king that 'merchants of Portugal and Lisbon may come safely into Ireland with wines and other merchandise ... and likewise merchants of Ireland may freely go ... to Portugal and Lisbon'. From this time onwards trade developed but, as in England, it is likely that Iberian wine took a small share of the market in the fourteenth and fifteenth centuries. Of two corn export permits for 1386-7, one mentions that the grain may be carried to Gascony or Spain and another that sixty crannocks of wheat from Co. Dublin may be brought to Portugal or Gascony. In 1405 a merchant of Kinsale paid local customs for eighteen tuns of Spanish wine in Chester.[7] A wine ship from Portugal in 1446 and one from Spain in 1449 were plundered off the south of Ireland, and a ship carrying Spanish wines was wrecked off Portmarnock, Co. Dublin, in December 1456.

For geographical reasons it seems likely that a good proportion of the wine from Spain and Portugal came in through the ports of the west coast, these being on a direct sailing route with the Iberian ports, and the oft-mentioned connection between Galway and Spain must have begun in the fifteenth century.

An agreement between a group of merchants drawn up in Bristol in 1453 gives a good idea of a round trip bringing wine to the west of Ireland. The *Julian* of Bristol was loaded with merchandise in Bristol and sailed for Lisbon where the English products were sold and wine, honey and salt were taken on board. The ship sailed to 'legge de Breon' (unidentified) and Galway where the wine, honey and salt were exchanged for hides. The ship then sailed for Flanders, where the hides were to be sold, via Plymouth, Winchelsea and Sandwich, but owing to various mishaps the cargo had to be disposed of at the latter port.[8] A similar trip must have been planned by the ship of Dartmouth chartered in Flanders by English merchants to carry goods from Spain to Ireland (1402). This ship was unsuccessfully attacked by certain Irishmen but the crew turned the tables on the attackers

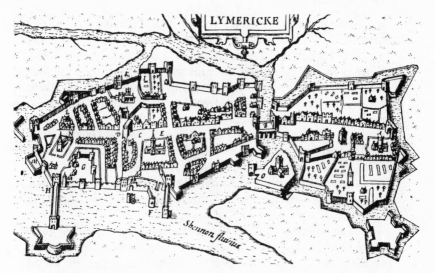

7 *Limerick, c.* 1600 (John Speed, *The theatre of the empire of Great Britain*, London, 1611)   The city was described by Stanihurst in 1577 as having 'sumptuous and substantial buildings' and a quay where ships of 200 tons might berth.

and were paid £400 ransom in Galway for the release of the captured Irish. Unfortunately, for the crew, however, they were set upon before leaving the port and deprived of the £400, together with £80 worth of merchandise. It would appear that a share of Spanish and Portuguese wine came in Bristol ships but Portuguese ships came also. There were two in Limerick in 1475, each with over fifty tuns of 'fine Portuguese wines called Oseys'.

The Bretons were appearing in increasing numbers in Irish waters from the mid-fifteenth century and, though salt and iron were their main cargoes, they also carried French wines. Three Breton ships, each over sixty tuns and laden with white Rochelle wine, were in Limerick in 1475.[9] One came with wine to Galway in 1503, but in general Breton ships kept more to the south-eastern and eastern ports and were sometimes chartered by Drogheda merchants. The act of 1485 which prohibited the import of Gascon wine, except in English, Irish or Welsh ships, does not appear to have had much effect in the Irish Sea area, as many Breton ships appear in the customs accounts of the north Welsh ports, paying prisage on their wines in Beaumaris and elsewhere in the later fifteenth century.[10]

The transit of the wine   Every voyage was regulated by a personal
contract between the merchant and the ship's master. Agreement was
reached as to cargo, freight charge and destination, with infinite
variations to suit particular circumstances. When some merchants
of Chester planned in 1393 to send a ship to Bordeaux or La Rochelle
for wines to be brought back to Ireland, they stipulated that the ship
must be unladen and reladen in Gascony within twenty-one days of
arrival. On the return journey the ship was to go to Dalkey and stay
there for three or four days, while the merchants decided whether
or not to go to Drogheda. John Motte, a citizen of London, freighted
the *Patrick* of Waterford in Drogheda in 1449 to sail, according to
the charter party agreement, to Bordeaux and return either to Dublin
or Drogheda.

There was always a degree of uncertainty about medieval voyages
and the hazards of wind, weather or war were very real considerations.
The decision regarding the port of destination might not be taken
till the return voyage had begun. In 1387 three Hanseatic merchants
in a German ship, with a Prussian master, had loaded fifty-one tuns
of wine at La Rochelle to bring to either England or Ireland. They
had, seemingly, opted for Ireland but 'by lack of skill of the lodesman
dared not steer the ship on the high sea towards Ireland'. So they
went into Falmouth to get a steersman familiar with Irish waters —
only to be attacked and robbed. The *Magdeleyne* of Drogheda was
heading home from Bordeaux to Drogheda in 1340 with wines and
other goods, when she was driven by a storm up the west coast and
had to unload in Galway. In 1403, the *George* of Milford, en route
from Lisbon to Dartmouth ended up in Waterford owing to bad
weather.[11]

Piracy and attack by enemy ships of war were always a great
threat, which led the English to organise the wine fleets to sail in
convoy during the Hundred Years' War — the long conflict between
England and France, 1337-1453. But the coasts of France and Brittany
were always feared by merchant shippers. In 1296 it was stated that
'the king desires that ships may sail for Gascony sometimes more
and sometimes less . . . that the masters may be sworn to keep to the
open sea without approaching the coasts of France or Brittany, on
account of perils which might arise'.

Some of the dangers on the first stage of the wine route, may be
seen in the case of a ship, *Le Riche de Colet*, en route for England
in 1305 with wine from Gascony. She was seized near St. Mathieu
in Brittany by pirates, who killed the crew of sixteen and sailed off
to Dundalk with the sixty seven tuns of wine aboard. On arrival,

however, the malefactors were arrested and a number of them hanged.[12] Consequently ships that were heading directly back to Ireland or to ports in the west of England and not calling for salt at The Bay, near the Loire estuary, probably kept well out to sea to avoid the Breton coast and the Scilly Isles, and turned east when their crews were sure of a clear run up St. George's Channel with the westerly winds.

After having giving Brittany a wide berth the wine ships entered the area sometimes referred to nowadays as the Celtic Sea, where more hazards were provided by 'pirates' of one sort or another, both Irish and English. The *Spiritus Sanctus*, a wine ship of Portugal coming to Ireland in 1446, was captured and brought to Ilfracombe, where the thirty-three tuns of wine she contained were disposed of. In 1404 Galf Callan of Dublin, sailing out to Bordeaux in his new ship of 100 tuns, was driven to Cornwall by a storm and his goods and ship were seized. In 1449 a Bristol fishing boat captured a Spanish ship laden with wine, iron and salt off the Cork coast, only to be set upon by a small fleet from Kinsale and deprived of its prize. The *St. John* of Bayonne with a cargo of wine and iron was overtaken and robbed by a Bristol ship 'near the coasts of Ireland' in 1457.

Thus the length of time taken by the voyage home varied greatly owing to factors outside the control of the shippers. In addition, delays and rough seas affected the quality of the wines. The *Grace Dieu* of Coleraine, a ship of Richard de Burgo, earl of Ulster, on its way home from Gascony in 1315, put into Falmouth where it was arrested and held for so long that the wines went bad. Sometimes the first part of the voyage might go well, only to end disastrously. Wines destined for the king in Scotland in 1307 left Bordeaux about 13 October and by November had been transferred to another ship at Dalkey, to be carried to Skinburness. But 'by the wildness of the sea, the ship was cast hither and thither', and when it came to land about the feast of Epiphany (6 January) the wines had gone bad.[13]

The arrival of the wine On arrival at the pre-arranged port the first requirement was to pay the tax known as the 'prise of wine'. The *recta prisa* or prise of wine was an ancient custom by which the king exacted one tun of wine from every ship arriving in England or Ireland with less than twenty tuns of wine, and two tuns from ships laden with twenty or more tuns, paying the merchants 20s. for each tun. By the *nova custuma* agreement of 1303, alien merchants paid 2s. instead, for every tun they imported. In Ireland the Butlers, earls of Ormond, took this prise 'from time out of mind'. The prise was not to be taken from ships that were in port sheltering from storms. This ruling was necessary: Irish merchants complained in 1357 that, whilst sailing to Ireland, they were often driven by storms to ports in Wales and Cornwall, and were compelled to pay prise not only in these places, but also when they came home.[14]

Sometimes wine ships on reaching the Irish Sea, touched at several ports where some of the wine was sold. In this case the prise was to be paid at the first port of call. A ship of Howel ap Phelip of Wales was held for not paying prise in Drogheda in 1355-7, but Howel claimed that he had paid the prise at Milford, a port in South Wales. The Mary of Guernsey, shipping Gascon wine to Chester in 1397-8, paid the prise when she called at Dublin. In 1414 two merchants protested when prisage was charged in Chester after they had paid it in Dublin. Payments of prise by Irish shippers of Gascon wine are recorded at Chester in 1394-5, 1396-7 and 1399. It is not possible to say whether these merchants unloaded all of the wine at Chester, or continued across to Dublin or Drogheda with part of it.[15]

Dublin port had difficulties in the middle ages caused by silting and it could not take the great ships laden with wines or other merchandise. Consequently ships had to unload, partially at least, at Dalkey, some three miles south of the Liffey mouth. The fact that the prisage could be paid there, or at Carnan within the precinct of the city, led to frequent disputes.[16]

The cost of the transit of the wine from France or Spain was considerable. Freight charges amounted to between 10 per cent and 12 per cent of the wholesale price, and increased gradually throughout the fourteenth and fifteenth centuries owing partly to inflation but mainly to war, for during escalations in the Hundred Years' War armed men had to be carried on voyages for the protection of merchants, ships and cargoes.

Although this overseas freight charge was by far the greatest, numerous other small charges added to the price of wine. There is a particularly good account for Dublin in 1332-3 which, in listing various expenses, tells us much about the work involved in shipping a consignment of wine. It describes the loading of a ship with wine, which was destined for the king in Scotland, and from the details a clear picture emerged of a large number of people at work in a medieval Irish port. On 23 March 1332, 100 tuns of wine were handed over into the care of John de la Bataille, the king's purveyor, for him to arrange shipment to Skinburness. Almost ten weeeks later, on 29

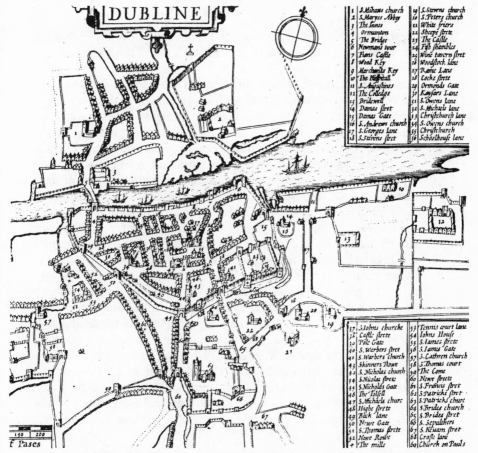

8 *Dublin, c. 1600* (John Speed, *The theatre of the empire of Great Britain*, London, 1611) Speed's plan shows some development had taken place outside the walls of the medieval city. The quay where boats were unloaded by the great crane was situated about half-way along the fortified waterfront.

May, 67 tuns were delivered to the keeper of the king's stores at Skinburness. The shortfall of 33 tuns was accounted for as follows: 21 tuns, 1 pipe were sold to cover expenses and realized £38 16s.; 5 tuns, 1 pipe were lost at sea in a bad storm; and 6 tuns were allowed for ullage; i.e. loss by leakage or absorption.

This is how the £38 16s. were spent. The hire of cellars under Holy Trinity Church (Christ Church), where the wine was stored from 23 March to 7 April, i.e. for 16 days at 2s. a week, cost 4s. The carriage of 77 tuns, 2 pipes from the cellars to the Quay was

organised by Nicholas de Brystoll and his fellow carriers, who charged
3d. a tun, or 1½d. a pipe (total 19s. 6d.). Next the hiring of two
barges to carry the wine out to the ship, the *Margaret of Goseford*,
which was anchored at Carnan, cost the same as the carriers (19s.
6d.). The hoisting of the wine with a windlass (Wyndag') on board
the barges cost 2d. a tun or 1d. a pipe (total 13s.) and the same amount
again was needed to get the wine on board the *Margaret*. As the
Margaret does not appear to have been a regular wine ship, but was
more than likely requisitioned, extra work had to be done to secure
the wine in the hold. For this John de la Bataille bought 'stillage
frames' to hold the tuns (10s.), 6 wooden beams at 10d. each (5s.)
1,900 nails (3s. 9d.), rope (1s. 3d.) and 7½ dozen hoops to strengthen
the barrels for the voyage (5s .5d.). The hire of a carpenter for one
day to cut the wood cost only 3d. while 2s. was spent on the hire
of a boat to bring the timber, nails, etc. out from the city to Carnan.
Other minor expenses includes 11d. 'for the carriage of 12 rundlets
to the barges to be taken to the ship for ullage of the said wines';
1s. 6d. for 9 pounds of Paris candles (*candelar' de Parys*) for those
who were guarding the wine during the night, and for 'stillage' of
the ship at Carnan, 6s.8d. The freight of the ship to Scotland, with
its 77 tuns 2 pipes, was 5s. a tun (£19 10s.). The skipper, Laurence
Lodeman, was paid 15s.4d. and the unloading of 67 tuns on the
quayside at Skinburness cost 11s.1d. John the purveyor himself was
paid 2s. 6d. a day for 67 days (£8 7s. 6d.) and the balance of the
£38 16s. amounted to £4 6s. 3d., which he paid into the treasury.[17]

Retail and distribution of the wine   It is difficult to be definite about
the wholesale price of wine during the period, as the variations seem
to have been enormous. About 1287, according to the sworn evidence
of merchants, a tun of wine was worth 28s. 8d., after the deduction
of freightage and other expenses. Allowing for expenses, wine could
not then have sold for much more than £2 a tun. In the early
fourteenth century the wholesale price of wine was about £3 a tun,
whereas the market value of a tun of wine may have been as high
as £4 13s. 4d. or even £6.[18] Spanish wine for the royal household
c. 1450, averaged £4 the tun for red wine and £8 for sweet.

Retail prices were fixed by law and so we can be more certain about
them. In general Irish prices varied little from those of England, as
the following examples show:

1306	Dublin	3d. (per gallon)
1329-31	Dublin	4d.
c. 1330	London	4d.
1381-2	Drogheda	8d. Red Gascon wine
1391	London	8d.
c. 1422	London	6d.
1470	Ireland	8d. Gascon
1470	Ireland	6d. Rochelle
1470	Ireland	10d. Spanish[19]

These prices are a fair guide. Sometimes retailers were prosecuted for overcharging: a Dublin taverner was selling wine at 6d. and even 8d. a gallon in 1315-16. Then, as now, the quality of the wine must have affected the price. According to their account book (c. 1340) the community of Holy Trinity, Dublin, bought wine in bulk, but perhaps that which they purchased in smaller quantities from retailers in Winetavern St. was of better quality. In 1343 they paid 6d. a gallon for white wine when the archbishop of Dublin was visiting the house. Spanish wine and sweet wines from the Mediterranean, when available, were always dearer. There is one reference in 1296 to German wine, when twelve hogsheads of Rhenish white wine were taken from John FitzRalph of Kilmallock for the king's use.[20]

The fortunes of the Hundred Years' War caused wine prices to fluctuate in England. In 1449 the price of a gallon of wine jumped to 10d. Throughout most of the fifteenth century, however, the price remained at 8d a gallon.

The transport of wine inland was never easy and always added to the cost. English retailers were allowed to add ½d. a gallon for every twenty-five miles and 1d. a gallon for every fifty miles the wine travelled (c. 1360). Whenever possible rivers were used and there were frequent complaints about weirs obstructing boats on the Barrow, Nore, Liffey and Boyne. Waterford's large share of medieval Irish wine imports was due to its situation in a safe harbour on the south-east coast of Ireland, making it a convenient first port of call for wine ships heading into the Irish Sea. It also enjoyed great advantages in the distribution of wine (and the collection of bulky commodities such as wool and hides) through the Suir, Barrow and Nore river system. It is quite likely that Matthew O'Mukian, the unedifying abbot of Holy Cross, Tipperary, who in 1488 was reproached for his involvement in the wine trade, received his goods via the river Suir, on which his abbey was situated.

John Blake, a merchant of Galway, must have faced a difficult journey overland when bringing wines to Roscommon *c.* 1460. A letter of about this date in Latin, and so most probably from an Irish chieftain, requests him to bring the wine to his town of Roscommon ... 'and if he can fix a day the writer will come and bring the cloth which he holds for him'. Other Galway merchants carried on trade with the local Irish, receiving hides in exchange for wine. Overland transport of merchandise would have been by pack horse and a sixteenth century source mentions that 'the manner of carrying wine in Ireland is in little barrels on horses' backs'.[21]

Some wine was reshipped along the coast from Dublin and Drogheda to Ulster. In 1402-3 two permits were issued to Dublin merchants, one for bringing nine tuns of wine and some merchandise to Lough Foyle and Lough Swilly. The second was for bringing six tuns of wine and six of ale and one *pakte* of bread to Lough Foyle and Assaroe in Ulster and freely selling them there. The amounts are small and it is very unlikely that the Ulster Irish were depending much on wine coming from Drogheda and Dublin. It would seem that shipments like these were connected with payments for fishing rights. It is likely that the twenty tuns of wine that were washed ashore near the mouth of the Erne in 1310 were lost from a passing wine ship. Visits from merchant ships became usual with the development of trade in fish.

The Ulster Irish may also have received wine through Sligo, which was visited by Bristol ships, and whose wine and other trading was the subject of an enquiry in 1425. No doubt large quantities of wine were drunk at feasts such as that held by Margaret O'Connor Faly (1451), and Holinshed recounts that Shane O'Neill was reputed to have had 200 tuns of wine in his cellar at Dungannon.[22]

Date	Ship	Bordeaux to -	Price per tun
1333	*St Marie* of Ipswich	Dublin	12s. 6d.
1334	*Bonan* of Bristol	Hull	10s. 0d.
1339	*St James* of Dartmouth	Dalkey	14s. 6d.
		Drogheda	21s. 0d.
		Chester	22s. 0d.
1394-5	*Trinity* of Ottermouth	Waterford	14s. 0d.
		Dublin	15s. 0d.
		Drogheda	16s. 0d.
		Beaumaris	18s. 0d.
		Chester	18s. 0d.
1499	*Bartholomew* of Bristol	Dublin	21s. 0d.
		Malahide	21s. 0d.
		Drogheda	21s. 0d.

II

Clothing

With the arrival of the Anglo-Normans came a great development in farming practice in Ireland. They introduced in the areas they colonised the manorial system and triennial crop rotation, which led to a great expansion of tillage. Extensive sheep farming was another vital element of the Anglo-Norman rural economy producing wool for export to the cloth industries of Europe. Great herds of sheep were also kept by the Cistercians, established in Ireland since 1142. These monks had been the first to organise wool exports from England and had developed sheep farming in Ireland on their monastic estates, which were often situated in limestone areas providing excellent grazing for sheep.

The scale and extent of the wool trade in thirteenth-century Ireland are clearly shown in the returns of the *Great Custom*, which was first collected in 1275. This custom was granted by the magnates to the king and amounted to a half mark (6s. 8d.) on every sack of wool exported, the same on a sack of woolfells and one mark on 200 hides. For customs purposes wool was reckoned by the sack, which was a standard weight of 364 lbs. of shorn wool, representing the clip of about 250 sheep. Most wool exported was shorn, but there was also a market for unshorn sheepskins, or woolfells, which were reckoned at 300 to the sack before 1368 and 240 later.[1]

Customs officials were appointed at every port in the land and were effectively supervised by Italian merchant bankers, to whom the taxes were going in repayment of the king's debts. Taxation and custom duties, such as the extra £2 a sack imposed on wool exports in 1294, were the only way that Edward I could pay back the enormous sums he borrowed for his military campaigns. These Italians were also great wool exporters and organised shipments from England and to a lesser extent from Ireland to the continent. They represented the banking firms of the Riccardi of Lucca and, after their collapse in 1294, the Frescobaldi of Florence and because they acted as official papal tax collectors they handled considerable amounts of liquid funds. With these assets they held a virtual monopoly of the wool trade at that time and were able to commandeer a high proportion of the annual wool clip through advancing loans against the wool. Apart from the king, many noblemen and religious houses in England and Ireland were deeply in debt to the Italians, particularly at times when disease, weather or war decimated the flocks.

Roger Bigod, earl of Norfolk and absentee landlord of estates in Co. Wexford, owed the king's bankers, the Riccardi, nearly £1,000 in the later thirteenth century. Sheep farming was an important part of the economy of his manors at Ballysax, Forth and Old Ross, where at the latter he had 1,894 sheep in 1289. Recent analysis of the Bigod estate accounts suggests that sheep were kept not only for their wool but also for manuring the fields to the benefit of corn production, which was the major source of income.[2]

Among the religious houses in Ireland in the later thirteenth and early fourteenth centuries, which came under pressure from the Italian bankers for loans not repaid, was the Cistercian monastery of Abington, Co. Limerick. In 1294 the abbot had to hand over to the Riccardi for fifteen years the income from the church and lands that the monastery held at Thurles. Some years later nearby Athassel Abbey, the largest medieval monastery in the country, also had to lease churches to pay off debts and the great Cistercian Abbey of Duiske at Graiguenamanagh, Co. Kilkenny, had agreed in 1299 to pay £100 in wool annually in settlement of debts owed to the Riccardi.[3]

It is not possible to calculate how much wool was exported in proportion to woolfells or hides, since the great Custom returns make no distinction between the commodities. Most Irish wool was sent to the great cloth manufacturing centres of Flanders. There are records of Irish wool being taxed at Bruges in 1273 and in 1300. The Irish wool was much coarser than the English, as the earliest Flemish drapery regulation from Bruges in 1282 clearly implies. This ranked cloths in accordance with their quality and required those made from English wools to be sealed with three crosses, from Scottish wools with two crosses, from Irish wools with one cross and from local Flemish wools with a half cross. The Irish wool was used for making less expensive cloth, probably mixed with wools of higher quality. The export continued throughout the fourteenth century. In the fifteenth century wool was exported to the Low Countries, mostly through the port of Calais. A local law of Leyden in 1423 forbade the import of Scottish, Irish, Flemish or any wool not purchased from the official English staple at Calais.[4]

In the thirteenth and early fourteenth centuries most Irish wool exports were managed by the Italian merchant bankers, who hired whatever shipping was convenient to convey the wool to Flanders. The shipmasters of the Hansa were sometimes engaged in this trade, as is implied by a sea law of Lubeck dating from *c.* 1300. Here it is stated that, when a ship sailed from England or Ireland, each crewman was to be allowed free stowage of a sack of wool. Shippers of wool from Ireland to the Continent frequently encountered difficulties with customs officials in the Channel ports of England, as did the merchants taking hides. The instance of the two shiploads delayed in 1338 is probably typical. One of them, consisting of twenty-three sarplars (about forty-six sacks) loaded at Waterford by Byndus Mask, a representative of the Bardi, was arrested in Sandwich and held for two years; some of the wool eventually went to Antwerp. The second shipment of twenty-six sarplars was also loaded at Waterford and was customed and cocketed to be taken to Zeeland or Brabant. The ship carrying this wool, the *Maryote* of Ross, was arrested and taken to Sandwich, where protracted negotiations eventually secured its release. A group of Dublin merchants found themselves in a similar predicament at Weymouth in 1341, but they also were allowed to proceed to Gascony or Flanders.[5]

The demand for Irish wool in England was not very great. A large consignment of about fifty sacks, which Robert Droup of Cork and others took to Plymouth and Dartmouth in 1356, still remained unsold five years later. 'Merchants refused to buy it because of its poor quality', the Irish merchants claimed, and so they were allowed to reship it to Flanders.[6] Coventry, the great centre of cloth manufacture, imported Irish wool to make 'Coventry frieze', a cloth like Irish frieze. Good profits were made on this rough cloth, since neither import duty was paid on the wool nor subsidy charged on the finished cloth. There was a sizeable number of Irish spinners and weavers working in the prosperous Coventry textile industry in the later fourteenth century. Coventry's imports of Irish wool probably came through Chester, although neither the Bristol nor the Chester customs accounts have records of Irish wool arriving in the fourteenth and fifteenth centuries. Both ports, particularly Bristol, imported large quantities of 'shorlings', or clipped sheepskins, and occasionally lambskins, but these cannot be taken as wool exports. Waste wool clippings or 'flock' were sometimes included in cargoes to Bristol from Ireland. A quantity of this poor quality wool, also called 'cog wool' or 'refus', arrived in Calais from Ireland in 1364 in the *Peter of Liverpool*.[7]

All the available evidence suggests that the great wool producing area of medieval Ireland was the south-eastern region. The bulk of the wool exports left from Waterford and Ross.[8] Both these ports were conveniently situated on the estuaries of a river system that passed through south Leinster and south-east Munster and provided a convenient transport system for bulky commodities such as wool and hides. The Suir, Nore and Barrow also flowed through the lands of ten major Cistercian abbeys, thus facilitating the transportation of their wool crop. On the Nore, for example, shallow draught barges could float from Kilkenny to New Ross in a day. Thomastown, only ten miles downstream from Kilkenny, was an important depot for hides and wool, and a number of late medieval store-houses still stand close to the river in the town.

By no means did all the wool exported come from the estates of the monasteries or the lands of the wealthy lords, nor was it all exported by the Italians. In Ireland, as in England, a great amount of wool must have come from the smaller flocks of lesser farmers and peasants, who would have sold it in the nearest town. The local wool merchants would in turn sell in bulk to the exporters, since foreign merchants were forbidden, in New Ross and in other towns, to buy goods directly from the producers. John le Blond of Kilkenny gave nine sacks of wool to another merchant in New Ross in 1305. John was a member of a wealthy merchant family (related to the Kytelers of Kilkenny), another member of which, Adam le Blond of Callan, could afford to lend the king £500 in 1303. Giles de Courtray of Bruges was one of several Flemings who had wool and hides stored in Kilkenny and Thomastown in 1295, presumably destined for export through Waterford and Ross. In 1319 several merchants witnessed the weighing and purchase of 15 sacks of wool in Clonmel for Thomas Mustard of Bristol, which were then freighted downstream to complete customs formalities in Waterford before being loaded on a ship bound for Bordeaux.[9] Waterford had evidently introduced some unusual regulations regarding the weighing and lading of wool, which caused foreign merchants to complain in 1355, but as will be seen Waterford wool merchants were to become involved in a much more serious legal quarrel in the fifteenth century, which was to have far reaching effects on Anglo-Irish relations.

There are scattered references to wool exports from other ports, for example, Carrickfergus and Cork. Some Scottish wool was brought

to Ireland and was probably re-exported. John de Leycester, a citizen of Dublin, sold victuals in Skinburness, the port of Carlisle, in 1379 and got six sacks of wool in return. Wool was one of the principal commodities that Scotland could offer to merchants in exchange for vital supplies of provisions and arms.[10]

Legislation governing the sale and export of wool and hides: the staple The main source of royal income was taxation of exports and wool was the commodity most heavily burdened in the later thirteenth century. After the sharp fall in wool exports in the 1290s associated with the fall of the Riccardi, tax and customs legislation, much of it aimed at the Frescobaldi and Bardi, successors of the Riccardi, developed after 1300 and let to the setting up of the staple. The staple was a fixed place through which the exports of wool, woolfells and hides were compulsorily directed. There were two kinds of staple: home and foreign. The first compulsory foreign staple was set up in St. Omer in 1313. Home staples were set up in 1326 and these included Dublin, Drogheda and Cork as the staples for Ireland. Some time between 1326 and 1355 Waterford was added to these.[11]

The arrangement of the staple was advantageous to both king and native merchants. For the king it could be, and was, applied as a diplomatic lever, for example to induce the Flemish towns to support the English side in the Hundred Years' War. It was also convenient for taxation purposes. For the native merchants, wool dealers, clothiers and clothmakers, the staple ordinance was a means of destroying the competition of foreigners in almost every branch of the wool trade.

According to the regulations of the staple (1326) alien merchants were permitted to barter wools, hides and skins only at the staple. When their purchasers had been customed and sealed (with the cocket), they were to wait a further fifteen days before departing. Merchants were to be governed by the Law merchant and sales were to be made to aliens only at the staples. Merchant strangers were under the king's protection. Men of Gascony and Guyenne were to be treated as denizens. Merchants were not to conspire to lessen prices. Citizens were to use only cloth made in England, Ireland and Wales. Cloth could be long or short (i.e. in lengths of twenty-four yards or twelve yards). To encourage the cloth industry fullers, spinners and dyers were to be offered francise in the towns. The wool merchants were to have a mayor of the staple. Each town was held responsible for the conduct of its sailors abroad.[12]

From time to time, additions and amplifications were made to the ordinances. In 1332, for example, it was stressed that merchant strangers were not to buy wool at abbeys but only at the staple. The standard weight of London was to be kept and lawful gold money and 'legal coins of Tours' were to be current.

Merchants of Ireland often sought exemption from certain obligations of the staple. In 1354 they complained that alien merchants 'do not commonly come to trade in Ireland' and so they were allowed, after having fulfilled custom and cocketting formalities, to sell at the English staples. Again they complained that the price offered for hides in England was very poor, with the result that the king granted that for three years the merchants might take hides 'to such as would buy them' but not wool, woolfells or lead. A major difficulty for any merchants trading out of Ireland in the fourteenth and fifteenth centuries was that, when en route to the Continent, they would be pressed for second payment of customs if they called at an English port.[13]

The staples for Ireland were at Dublin, Drogheda, Cork and Waterford. This meant in practice that a merchant from Limerick or Galway had to undertake the dangerous coastal voyage to Cork with wool to complete the customs formalities before proceeding to the Continent. In 1375, 'for the relief of burgesses and merchants of the town of Galway . . . and other merchants of Connacht', Galway was granted a cocket seal, which enabled all customs to be paid in the town and ships to proceed directly to the Continent or to England. In 1377 the seal was removed and Galway merchants were obliged once more to travel to Cork for customs clearance.[14] It is extremely doubtful whether this regulation was always complied with. In 1415 a group of Galway merchants and one John O'Morchowe of Athenry expressed the far-fetched claim that, while on their way in a ship of Lubeck to pay customs, they were caught in a storm and ended up in Sluys. On returning to Galway, however, they promised to set aside the amount due in customs. Already in 1400 the staple of Calais was set up and all merchants of the king's dominions trading with the Continent were obliged to transact their business there — a precept that was frequently ignored. In 1416 another group of Galway merchants, this time shipping staple merchandise in a Portuguese vessel, were intercepted as they attempted to bypass the staple of Calais. Their goods to the value of 800 marks were held in Southampton.[15]

By this time the regulations of the staple had become more and more complex, reflecting against the background of the Hundred Years' War the conflicting interests of king, parliament, and native and foreign merchants. In 1429 the Irish parliament repudiated the claim of the English parliament that the legislature regarding the staple of Calais was binding upon Irish merchants. The Irish parliament enacted in that year that the citizens of the Irish boroughs 'are enfranchised and have liberties (having first paid their customs and cocket of our lord the king) of passing into Flanders, Zeeland and any other places and countries whatsoever beyond the sea to peoples friendly and at peace with out lord the king ... with staple and other merchandise and there selling them and bartering'. Although this act was passed in 1429, the question did not come into the courts until 1483. In that year certain merchants of Waterford, disregarding the English statute (as they must have done before), consigned a cargo of staple commodities, including wool, woolfells and hides, to Sluys in Flanders. The ship had to put into Calais and was there arrested. The merchants petitioned the king for restitution and their claim was referred to the judges. A long case resulted.[16] The merchants cited the rights of Waterford enshrined in the city charters, which, they claimed, no English parliament could derogate. In fact they asserted that an English Act was not binding in Ireland, a view upheld by the exchequer chamber. But the decision was given against the merchants, on the grounds that the merchants, as the king's subjects, were bound by anything done against the statute outside Ireland.

The matter did not rest there, as the merchants presented a second bill. This was heard in the first year of Henry VII (1485-6), when the chief justice is reported to have laid down that statutes made in England did bind the people of Ireland. The repudiation of the staple regulations by the Irish parliament and the case brought by the merchants of Waterford drew the attention of Henry VII to the anomalous relationship between the two governments and must surely have prepared the ground for the passing of Poynings' Law.

9 *Cloth seal of lead, c.* 1500 (National Museum of Ireland) This seal bearing the arms of Rouen, was found at Wood Quay, Dublin. Drawing (2:1) courtesy of P.F. Wallace, N.M.I.

The fortunes of the Irish wool merchants were closely bound up with those of their English counterparts. In fifteenth-century Ireland there was a decline in the export of raw wool, just as there was in England. This change may have been influenced by the decline in manorial farming in the south-eastern part of the country, which certainly affected corn growing in the area. It is more likely, however, that just as in England the wool crop was used to manufacture cloth, which was a much more profitable export than wool because the tax on wool exports was something in the region of 33 per cent while on cloth it was less than 5 per cent.

Little is known about how or where Irish cloth was manufactured in the middle ages, but it appears that there were two kinds of production. Some cloth was made in the country as a 'cottage industry', for family use and also as an item for sale or barter. In addition most of the larger towns would have had, as in England and elsewhere, a community of cloth workers spinning, weaving, dyeing and finishing cloth for retail and for export. It is clear from medieval wills and other sources that substantial amounts of linen were produced in the Galway area and used for barter in the town; in Limerick also merchants like Thomas Arthur were dealing in cloth produced by people of the hinterland.[1]

The production of good quality cloth required many different processes and a widespread division of labour, as is borne out by well-documented accounts from England and Europe. The scant records from Ireland imply that somewhat similar structures were employed. The wool was washed and prepared, carded and combed and then spun into yarn using distaff and spindle (the use of the spinning wheel was not widespread before 1500). By the thirteenth century the flat-bed loom, similar to what is used today, was widespread in western Europe. On it different qualities of cloth and different widths could be produced. After weaving, the cloth was washed and fulled, which involved pounding and beating in water containing either potash or alum (called fuller's earth), which made the cloth thicker. After more rinsing and drying the cloth was finished by being brushed with teasels and shorn. By then it needed stretching and shaping by tenterhooks before it could be sold. If the wool was not dyed in the yarn the cloth now went to the dyers, who produced a whole variety of colours using combinations of woad (blue), madder (red), saffron (yellow), or the very expensive red dyes — brazil, vermilion and *grana*. The dyers were highly skilled craftsmen and in Drogheda as early as 1329 they had their workshops in Dyer Street close to the River Boyne. Woad and saffron were imported through Bristol, as was alum, the mordant for fixing the dyes that came from the shores of the Black Sea and the eastern Mediterranean. Alum was expensive: a hundredweight was valued at £15 in 1471 when it was in storage in Drogheda for Richard Boys of Coventry, a cloth merchant living in Dublin.[2]

The maximum prices for the various processes in cloth production were fixed by the municipality of Dublin in the early fourteenth century. Carding wool was costed at 1d. a stone, weaving 300 ells of cloth of one colour at 16d.; weaving fine red cloth at ¾d. for each ell. Fulling 30 ells cost 3s. and fullers were paid 2d. a day. Waterford had similar price regulations and both cities had weavers guilds in the middle ages.

With the development of her own weaving industry, low priced woollen cloth became one of Ireland's important exports in the later middle ages. This cloth was of a rough napped quality generally classed as frieze or serge. England was the chief export market. Bristol received the largest quantities of Irish cloth, but Irish cloth was shipped to other ports as well. A list dating from c. 1300 of customs duties levied at Southampton notes that 2d. was to be paid on every hundred ells of Irish cloth and a list of tolls to be paid in Tenby in 1344 also mentions Irish cloth.[4]

Much of the Irish cloth exported to England was re-exported by both English and alien merchants. It is likely that Garcius Arnaud and other foreign merchants who shipped Irish cloth to Bristol in 1325-6 later took it to the Continent. Elias de Stubton, a citizen of Lincoln trading in Normandy in 1327, had among his goods Irish cloth valued at £20. Hanseatic merchants sometimes traded in Irish cloth. In 1360 a quantity of Irish cloth (*panni Irenses*) was shipped from Hamburg to Oslo. In 1378 a prohibition was directed against the merchants of the Hansa forbidding the export from England of unfulled cloth and 'friseware cloth made in Ireland or in England of Irish wools', because they were not of the statutory length and breadth. Merchants and shipmasters leaving Chester for Spain in the later fifteenth century often took packs of frieze as well as woollen cloth; it is likely that the frieze was Irish, or 'Coventry frieze' made in England from Irish wool.[5]

Irish cloth (as distinct from manufactured garments) was a valued material in later medieval Europe. An Italian poem of c. 1360, the

Dittamondo by Fazio degli Uberti, which includes the author's description of his travels in England, Scotland and Ireland, begins an account of Ireland thus:

> In like manner we passed into Ireland, which among us is worthy of renown for the excellent serges that she sends us (*per le nobile saie che ci manda*)

An entry in a Florentine account book of about the same date records expenditure for a piece of serge of Ireland (*saia d'Irlanda*) for clothing. In 1382 Cosmatas Gentilis, the pope's collector in England, was allowed to ship various fabrics tax-free from Bristol, including 'five mantles of Irish cloth, one of them lined with green cloth, another of mixed colour lined with green cloth, a garment (*indumentum*) of russet lined with Irish cloth . . .' Another example of Irish cloth being used for lining at this time comes from France. An entry in the accounts of the French royal household in 1389 mentions that a length of Irish serge (*sarge d'Irlande*) was purchased from a merchant in Paris and delivered to the king's tailor for the lining of two costumes.[6]

Linen yarn and cloth   Some time after 1400 the manufacture of linen cloth developed in Ireland. Previously flax was grown and yarn was exported to England, but the cloth was not manufactured here. In the fifteenth century linen exports became important and large shipments are recorded in the Bristol customs books — upwards of 20,000 yards were imported in one year. Irish linen was also being imported at Southampton. Irish linen was well known on the Continent in the fifteenth century and sales of Irish cloth (*tele*), most likely linen, were recorded at Avignon in 1432 and 1436.[7]

Little is known about local production. Kenneth Nicholls says that weaving was regarded as a degrading trade in Gaelic Ireland and quotes a remark of Conall Mageoghagan, the seventeenty-century translator of the Annals of Clonmacnoise: 'This Shane (O'Conor) was the son of a woman that could weave, which of all trades is the greatest reproach amongst the Irishry, especially the sons and husbands of such tradeswomen . . .'. As far as we can tell, linen was made in different parts of the country: Galway in particular seems to have been a centre of production from which linen was exported to the Continent. In 1492 Leonard Lynch of Galway sued James Adurnus, a merchant of Genoa, for the cost of 6,000 bales of linen cloth. The will of Valentine Blake, a burgess of Galway who died in 1499, indicates that he dealt in linen. A number of Irishmen, who are named, owed him several hundred linen cloths.[8]

Linen yarn continued to feature in trade. In 1481, in a dispute regarding customs in Dublin, James Welles, claiming to be a freeman of the city, refused to pay poundage on various goods, including 900 pounds of linen yarn. John Wilde, the Coventry cloth merchant who died in Dublin in 1471, also had linen yarn and cloth in his possession.

Linen cloth was produced in great quantities in the sixteenth century and many of the Elizabethan travellers noted the extravagant amounts used to make shirts and head-dresses. One Gaelic lord's shirt contained something between 30 and 40 yards of linen and a lady's kerchief or turban used 24 yards! This extravagance was condemned by statutes of the period. Yarn continued to be exported to supply English cloth manufacturers until the end of that century.[9]

Mantles The word 'mantle' is generally used to describe the capacious garment of coarse wool to which the closest modern equivalent would be a large *poncho*. Called in Irish *falling* and anglicised *falding*, it was the characteristic item of medieval Irish dress. An attempt to ban the wearing of mantles in Dublin was made in a municipal regulation of 1466. Regarded by the Elizabethans as barbaric apparel, their view is succinctly expressed by Spenser, who described it as 'A fitt house for an outlaw, a meete bedd for a rebell and an apt cloke for a thief'.[10]

The Irish mantle was well known in Britain and on the Continent from the time of the Celtic missionaries in the eighth century. A twelfth-century version of the Life of the early Welsh Saint, Cadog, refers to the 'many ringlets or tufts of his *coccula*, a certain type of garment which the Irish use out of doors, full prominent tufts or coils like hair'. A similar garment is the mantle of St. Brigid in Bruges. This is claimed to be of Irish origin, having been given to the Cathedral by the sister of Harold, the last Anglo-Saxon king of England. He had visited Leinster in 1051 and Brigid was the chief patron of Leinster.

In the fourteenth century, owing to greater demand for mantles, the native cloth industry began to expand. Irish sheep, like the Shetland breed today, grew long coarse fleeces, from which the heavy cloth for making mantles, rugs and faldings was woven. The mantles were manufactured in Ireland and sent to England, whence they reached the continental market. In 1377 Peter Slotelore of Flanders conveyed four 'mantles of Ireland', along with other goods, from London to Flanders. In 1378 Dedric Sadelar of Bruges purchased in London eleven dozen Irish mantles and Tideman Knyghtkyn, a

10 *The Irish mantle* This heavy
woollen garment was popular
at home and abroad. The
drawing is based on a sketch
by the German artist Dürer
(1471-1528).

German merchant, loaded in the same port that year two hundred
'faldynges' and one hundred yards of 'faldyngclothe' of Ireland to
take to his own country. London appears to have been a distribution
centre for Irish manufactured cloth and garments, and the trade was
most probably in the hands of mercers who had trading connections
in Ireland.[11] The mantles were popular with all classes, just as Aran
sweaters are today. Among the goods that the earl of Warwick had
with him in his prison in Tintagel Castle, Cornwall, in 1397 were
two Irish cloaks (*clamides*). The papal tax collector already referred
to had five mantles, two of which had coloured lining. About 1440
Archbishop Prene of Armagh sent to John Stafford, the bishop of
Bath and Wells and chancellor of England, a gift of an Irish frieze
cloak.[12]

The export of mantles was closely linked with the cloth trade,
Bristol taking the greatest number, and the Southampton Port Books
also note imports. Most of these would have come through Waterford,
which was the principal area of manufacture and distribution of
mantles and rugs. In the sixteenth century mantles were commonly
known as 'Waterford rugs'. Municipal regulations of the city in

1485-86 attempted to control this valuable trade and restricted 'sheremen, frizers or tesellers' from selling friezes and mantles to foreign merchants. In fact only the actual manufacturers of cloth were allowed to sell the same from their own houses. Interestingly these regulations coincide with the establishment of the weavers' guild in the city in 1485. By the sixteenth century the manufacture of cloth was an important industry and to safeguard supplies of wool an act was passed by the Irish parliament in 1522 forbidding the export of wool and 'flocks' out of the land.[13]

THE IMPORTATION OF ENGLISH CLOTH

Ireland, from the abundant supplies of native wool, produced more than enough woollen cloth to supply her own needs, with the result that the import of English cloth was more of a luxury than a necessity. English cloth, made from fine wool, was renowned all over Europe at this time for its quality. Lydgate, an English poet writing in the early fifteenth century, proudly proclaimed:

> All naciouns afferne up to the fulle
> In al the world ther is no better wolle.

English cloth came in a variety of qualities, weights and colours, but it was classed by customs officials simply as *panni sine grano, panni in dimidio grano*, and *panni in grano*, according to whether it was dyed without, partly with, or wholly with the expensive kermes dye ('grain'). Clothes in which kermes were used paid higher duty, on the assumption that they were of better quality. The other cloths were dyed with less expensive materials, or perhaps left undyed. Nevertheless the term *sine grano* ('without grain') does not mean, as is sometimes stated, undyed or unfinished cloth.

The fortunes of the export trade in English cloth and wool have been the subject of many scholarly studies and, when compared with the quantities of cloth shipped by Hansard and Italian merchants, the exports to Ireland appear to have been small. They were not insignificant, however, particularly the amounts shipped through

Bristol and Chester. Most imported cloth came to Ireland through these ports, although they were occasional direct imports from the Continent. The cloth trade with Bristol was long established, while that with Chester reached its full development towards the middle of the fifteenth century. As might be expected, Bristol's dealings were mainly with the ports of the southern coasts, whereas Chester's trade was concentrated in the Dublin-Drogheda area.[1]

Bristol The Bristol customs accounts have numerous references to cloth exports to Ireland, particularly in ships of Waterford and of Co. Cork, as can be seen in the analysis of these accounts recently presented by W.A. Childs. It is clear that Ireland took a significant share of Bristol's cloth exports in the later fourteenth century. This amounted to about 20 per cent in the 1370s and 25-30 per cent in the 1390s, representing 800-1,200 cloths and close to 6 per cent of England's annual cloth exports. Since cloth was a staple product, exports to Ireland were carefully controlled and customs disputes were not unusual. Geoffrey Blake, a merchant of Galway, was in trouble in 1395 regarding the illegal exportation of eight whole cloths.

More serious was the complaint made by the customs officials of Bristol that their method of cocketing cloth, which was approved in Bordeaux and other places in the king's dominions, was not accepted by the customers of Cork. The pattern of trade continued in the fifteenth century, with almost every Ireland-bound ship leaving from Bristol or its outport Bridgewater and carrying some cloth. The 1479-80 account records the departure of the *Marie* of Fuenterrabia (Spain), which was bound for Ireland with a large cargo of cloth shipped by Spanish, Bristol and Irish merchants, but it is not clear how often shipments of this nature left Bristol. As has been noted earlier, Bristol fishing boats visited the west of Ireland in increasing numbers from around 1400 and almost all carried some cloth which was to be exchanged for fish. The number of cloths exported diminished to an average of 400-500 a year towards the end of the century. Whether this was due to the development of Ireland's own cloth industry, or to an increase of imports through Chester, or to factors affecting the market in Bristol itself, remains unclear.

The general pattern of Irish trade with Bristol in the later middle ages appears to have been concerned mainly with Irish exports of fish in return for Bristol's cloth. This continued and increased in the early sixteenth century, and the 1504-5 account shows that the volume of trade to and from Ireland had almost doubled in ten years.

Further proof of increased Irish activity is evidenced by Star Chamber proceedings against the Redcliffe fair in 1529. At the hearing Bristol drapers, tailors and grocers complained that the Irish were ignoring them, dealing instead with merchant strangers and selling them fish to the detriment of the city of Bristol.[2]

Chester Coventry was the chief centre of cloth manufacture in the English midlands and had a close trading link with Ireland through the port of Chester during the later middle ages. A number of Coventry merchants, including John Assheburn, Richard Delahide and Richard Midnight, who shipped through Chester, were all freemen of Dublin. So too were John White, Christopher Hegly and Thomas Lang, who described themselves as merchants of England and Ireland. In 1480, in a customs dispute, they claimed that they could not reside permanently in Dublin since they had to be in England, buying and selling. Much earlier, in 1323-4, merchants of Chester complained that they were being treated as foreign merchants by the customs officials of Dublin and orders were given to have the matter rectified.

The cloth industry of Coventry used mainly local wool in its manufacture, but also quantities of Welsh and Irish wool. Much of the latter must have come through Chester, although the nature of the customs accounts makes it impossible to quantify either cloth exports or wool exports, since the figures are disguised in terms such as 'pack' or 'load'. An indication of the trade between Coventry and Ireland may be seen in the 1404 account. Here the origins of 207 and 331 merchants trading through Chester are given: of these 103 were from Coventry and 87 from Ireland, mainly from Dublin, Drogheda, Rush and Malahide. The wills and inventories of two Coventry merchants who lived in Dublin yield further evidence of this two-way trade, by which wool, yarn and dyestuffs went to Coventry and manufactured cloth was brought to Ireland in return. Richard Boys, who died in 1471, had unsold cloth worth £3, a supply of cloth in the house of John Broun of Navan 'otherwise of London', and seven and a half hundredweight of alum in Drogheda. Boys was also owed money by various people for cloth. John Wilde had linen cloth, yarn, sheep and lambskins in his possession when he died. Further details in both wills, particularly regarding the appointment of executors and overseers, indicate a sizeable 'colony' of Coventry merchants having business in Dublin, all connected with wool and cloth passing through the port of Chester.[3]

London was another source from which cloth came to Ireland. K. P. Wilson notes that, in a dispute between two Coventry merchants in 1438, a quantity of cloth freighted from London and bound for Dublin was seized at Oxford.

An overland trade route from Chester to London is suggested by a petition from the Irish Parliament to Henry VI in 1429, complaining that merchants and others from Ireland travelling 'fro Chester to Coventre Oxenford and Londonn' have been attacked and robbed of their goods and horses.[4] A number of London drapers and mercers appointed attorneys in Dublin and Drogheda to look after their interests. These attorneys were cloth merchants residing in Ireland. Several merchants named White of Dublin represented different London mercers, indicating perhaps that members of this family specialised in the cloth trade. Hugh White represented William Marcheford in 1397, John Oteleye in 1399 and John More in 1404. In 1419 John White was named as attorney for William Norton, a draper of London, and Henry White was the representative of John Washbourne in 1420. One Richard White, a tailor of Dublin c. 1450, held the archbishop's crozier (which contained the famous Bachall Ísu) in pledge for 5 marks![5]

11   *The mayors of Dublin, Waterford, Cork and Limerick* (*Facs. nat. Mss Ire.* IV, 4)   These drawings are reduced from coloured originals in the charter roll of the corporation of Waterford c. 1400.

A wealthy London cloth merchant with important business interests in Ireland and who is listed in the Chester accounts was James Welles. In 1458 he undertood to clear a debt of £500 which the archbishop-elect of Armagh, John Bole, had contracted with the Lombards of the Medici Bank of London. Welles paid the Lombards in cloth and in return had the income of the archbishop's manors of Termonfechin, Dromiskin and Kilmoon and the tithes of the town of Athboy until he received the £500 plus £51 6s. 6d. interest. It is not certain how long he remained in control of the manors, but he certainly had them seven years later in 1465.

Welles became the first master of the guild of English merchants trading in Ireland (called the Fraternity of the Blessed Virgin Mary), which was established in 1479 and incorporated by statute in 1481. The guild was the outcome of a bitter row between Dublin merchants and those of England, particularly men of London, Coventry and Chester. The quarrel flared up in 1460 when the Dublin municipality resolved to expel English merchants from the freedom of the city because they were clubbing together to prevent Dublin merchants from sending cargo on ships freighted by them. The English responded by seeking from the king a charter for a guild of their own in Dublin and by saying that Dublin men trading in England would be without protection in that country unless they joined. The Dubliners responded to this by declaring that any freeman of their city who joined the new English merchants' guild would automatically be fined and lose his privileges. An indication of the consequences of the dispute can be seen in an incident of 1481 when James Welles was involved in a customs dispute in Dublin. He was asked to pay poundage of £8 13s. 6d. on merchandise that included 900 yards of linen yarn and a quantity of fish, which he refused to do, claiming exemption as a resident (commorant of the city) of Dublin. A jury found him guilty and ordered that his goods and chattels be forfeited and that he be fined.[6]

The sale and distribution of cloth in Ireland The sale of cloth was governed by strict regulations. A number of statutes were passed that specified the lengths, breadths and prices of different varieties of English cloth, and municipal laws imposed further controls on sales. The charters of most Irish towns have a clause to the effect that no foreigner may retail cloth or remain in town with his wares for more than forty days. In 1383 the burgesses of Dundalk successfully defended this right against John Druming and other foreign merchants, who had initiated proceedings against the bailiffs of the town when these officials prevented them from selling or cutting their cloth.[7]

The sale of cloth was a feature of every fair and market throughout the period of this study and a number of incidental references infer that both native and foreign merchants participated. In 1284 a prominent Italian merchant was captured by the Powers of Waterford and he lost cloth to the value of twelve marks; in a similar incident near Wexford in 1334, Nicholas de Pickering was robbed of 40s. in money and linen and woollen cloth worth 60s. Shops were burgled in Cork in 1295 and from one, thirteen ells of cloth were taken. Henry de Norwych was in Cashel in 1303 with a cartload of merchandise that included seven ells of russet cloth worth fifteen shillings.[8]

Many of the English merchants who brought cloth to Ireland through Chester had trading connexions with the inland towns of the Pale, such as Ardee, Athboy, Kells, Navan and Trim, as well as with Dublin and Drogheda. Richard Boys of Coventry sold cloth to Matthew Russel of Trim and also had cloth stored in Navan. Gilbert Walker of Yorkshire sold a quantity of coarse cloth in Dublin to John Whitechurch of Trim in 1472-3 and James Welles secured an excommunication for John Ledwych of Kells in 1478 — an extremity sometimes resorted to for long outstanding debts. Whether these merchants travelled periodically from town to town we cannot be sure; they may have conducted their business from the ports.[9]

Good quality cloth was a highly valued commodity in the Gaelic areas and appears to have been a most acceptable gift in treaties and exchanges between important personages. An agreement between O'Neill and Archbishop Bole of Armagh in 1458, states that having sworn fidelity to the Church of Armagh, O'Neill is to receive annually two dozens* of common English cloth. According to the Annals of Ulster in 1463 'the king of the Saxons (Edward IV) sent ... eight and forty yards of scarlet and a collar of gold' to O'Neill. At the end of the fifteenth century presents of expensive cloth, including velvet, were made by Lord Deputy Poynings to various Irish chiefs and ecclesiastics.

Scattered references imply that the merchant from the town was

---

*A *dozen* was a cloth 14 yards long by 2 yards wide.

an occasional visitor to the households of the Gaelic chieftains, selling his wares and no doubt bearing gifts and intelligence back and forth. There appears to have been a political dimension to the visit of the merchant John Beek to Diarmuid MacMurrough Láimhdhearg, for at Easter 1376 John claimed that he was still owed 71s. by the king 'for English bread and clothes supplied to Diarmuid together with 31s. for one basin broken and 24s. for a worstead carpet damaged at a banquet of the said Diarmuid. Also, 16s. for leggs [*draps de liège*] for the said Diarmuid's use'. Thomas Arthur was a general merchant of Limerick who dealt in a variety of goods. Surviving documents show that he had stocks of 'leggs', silk, buckram, quantities of unspecified cloth and madder for dyeing. Among his debtors in 1426 were several members of the Mac Con Mara (Macnamara) and MacMathghamhna (MacMahon) Gaelic Irish families of Co. Clare, whose purchases included cloth.

A further example from the north-west tells the story of a Dublin merchant who was in Sligo visiting O'Connor, when a group came in and with a poem in honour of the chieftain. This they recited and were well paid. Later, when these men came to the merchant to buy arms and cloth, he asked them if they had any more poems for sale. They said they had and sold him one for £10. Shortly afterward the merchant returned to O'Connor and, in the hope of making some money, offered him the poem. He had been tricked, however, since the poem he had bought was more than a hundred years old. O'Connor Sligo, in a gesture of generosity, gave the merchant double what he had paid for it!

There seems to be little doubt that the cloth trade was particularly valuable in medieval Ireland and merchants prospered in all branches of the trade in this lightweight, portable, sometimes expensive but always essential commodity. In an Anglo-Irish satirical poem of *c.* 1308, the author points to the merchants' wealth gained from sales of wool and cloth:

> Hail be yer marchans with yur gret packes
> Of draperie auour de peise and yur wol sackes,
> Gold siluer stones riche markes and ek pundes
> Litil giue ye thereof to the wrech pouer.[10]

The export of hides was a major factor in the trade of medieval Ireland. Cow hides and calfskins were, next to fish, Ireland's most important export. Hides were exported from all parts of the country, in small quantities from the less important ports and havens and in large consignments from the quays of Drogheda, Dublin and Waterford. They were carried in small boats and in large Spanish and Hanseatic vessels by English and foreign merchants as well as by merchants from Irish ports. In general the bulk of Ireland's hide exports between 1300 and 1500 were destined for the markets of continental Europe. It is not possible, owing to the nature of the sources, to quantify these exports. Customs records after 1300 are scant and unspecific and, even for the later thirteenth century when the figures appear relatively full, the returns were made without distinguishing between the taxable commodities: wool, hides and sheepskins. Available figures c. 1275 - c. 1345, tabulated by Gearóid Mac Niocaill, can give no idea of the actual amount either of hides or of wool exported, but can serve as indicators of the magnitude of the general export trade.[1]

A sizeable number of references in the calendars of patent and close rolls testifies to a varied export trade in hides. Although most of the entries from these sources refer to disputes about customs payments in English ports, whither ships had resorted owing to bad weather, pirates or war, they give details that indicate a regular and extensive trade in hides between Ireland and the Continent, especially Flanders, in the fourteenth and fifteenth centuries.

A typical entry of this nature would be the case of William White and Robert Lowys, both of Dundalk, who in 1339 loaded 1,000 hides in the *Laurence* of Drogheda and having paid the custom in Drogheda, sailed for Antwerp. Because of the king's enemies the ship was forced to come to London, where the hides were seized and William and Robert asked to pay customs again. They protested at this and instructions came from the king to check their letters of cocket.* If these letters were in order the two men were to be allowed to proceed to Antwerp in a ship not chosen for the king's service.[2]

In such cases considerable delay must have been caused by the

---

*The cocket was a seal belonging to customs officials. Letters of cocket were sealed by them and given to merchants testifying that duty had been paid on their goods. Hides were taxed at 13s. 4d. (1 mark) per 200.

necessity to send a petition to the king and to await the royal mandate. In 1370 William Canynges of Bristol was taking 12,000 hides from Ireland to the staple at Calais when his 'little ships' were forced into Bristol by bad weather. When the hides were unloaded they were seized by the customs officials and Canynges had to petition for an order of release.

One difficulty that arose with the customs authorities was that hides, on being unloaded in England, might be sold there despite having been customed for Flanders. John Barstaple of Bristol was on his way from Limerick to Calais with 2,400 hides in 1390 when storm damage forced him to reload on to a safer ship in Bristol. He was granted leave to proceed, provided that the Irish letters of cocket were in order and that he had not exposed the hides for sale in Bristol.[3]

It would appear, however, that the trade in hides between Ireland and England in the later middle ages was inconsiderable. This may have been due partly to lower prices on the English market. In 1436, when the ship of John Churche with its cargo of hides from Ireland was arrested in Southampton for the king's service, he and the other merchants were granted leave to have the hides stored there and reloaded when the ship was free again. They claimed that they would lose money if they sold the hides in England. In the Bristol customs accounts only occasional small consignments of hides are shown as coming from Ireland.

In the 1479-80 account, one of the most comprehensive available, it is shown that only 950 hides, worth approximately £63, were imported that year. The needs of Bristol's leather industries were supplied by Welsh hides. Similarly the fifteenth-century Chester customs accounts show that hides were well down the list of imports from Ireland. Fish, woad, woollen cloth were the chief imports in the earlier part of the century, followed by hides, yarn and lambskins; later, while fish retain top place and corn was becoming more important, hides still represent a small proportion of the total trade. These small shipments suggest a little trading by the crew members of ships to England rather than by the merchants themselves and this is further borne out by the Black Book of the Admiralty, which states (c. 1400) that a sailor's wages between Ireland and London were to be ten shillings and the carriage of thirty hides.[4]

Irish hides went instead to Gascony, in exchange for wine, but the main market was Flanders. Here there was a constant demand for leather to supply the needs of the prosperous large towns of the area, which had become one of the chief manufacturing regions of medieval Europe. Great quantities of Irish hides also went to Pisa where, for example in six months during 1466-7 nearly 34,000 were imported and 24,000 over the same period in 1482-3. These shipments may have gone to Italy from Flanders through the well-established trade route via the Rhone valley and Avignon.

Good profits could be made on hides, which fetched £18 a last (200) in Flanders according to a fifteenth-century merchant's handbook, and this represents about a thirty per cent profit on the buying price in Waterford (see below). Returns like this meant that major shipments of hides were taken to Flanders and Gascony from the bigger Irish ports in large continental merchant ships. In 1353 Robert More, William White, Elias de Preston and John Dyere, all of Drogheda, shipped 3,700 hides in a Spanish ship, which put in at Southampton on its way to Flanders to await a favourable wind. In 1382 John Toky of Limerick loaded 13,000 to take them to Flanders in a ship of Sluys.

Generally a group of merchants would combine to organise a cargo and charter a large ship. In 1415 five Galway merchants and three from Athenry together shipped hides from Galway to Sluys in a ship of Lubeck. A group of Drogheda merchants were involved in an unusual incident in their home port in 1384. They had loaded 12,225 hides on to three ships for export, but found themselves left behind and the hides stolen. The cargo had been put in the *Seyntemarie Knyght* of Gdansk, the *Christofre* of Campe (in Flanders) and the *Kateryne* of Bristol. Sailors on the *Seyntemarie* and the *Christofre* had expelled the Drogheda men, robbed the *Kateryne* and sailed away, leaving the Drogheda men very much poorer.[5]

Merchants frequently engaged in a coastal trade in hides by calling at several ports in order to make up a cargo. In contrast to the large shipments that have been referred to above, this coastal trade generally involved smaller consignments of hides. In 1340 Robert de Wryngton and two companions had brought and customed 610 hides at Galway, Carrickfergus and Waterford. That same year William Gilbert and others applied in Southampton for new letters of custom for 460 bought in Waterford, Wexford and Youghal, and which they were taking to Flanders or Gascony. A good example of coastal trading is the case of the *Seinte Antoyne* of Spain, which was freighted in 1360 by Bristol merchants. It was arrested en route to Flanders on suspicion of customs evasion and escorted to Dartmouth. The investigation of the letters of cocket showed that the ship had taken on hides at Dublin, Waterford and Cork. It called at Carmarthen in Wales for wool and at Bristol for wool, hides and other merchandise.[6]

It is possible that a section of this coastal trade in hides was connected with fishing and William Canyngs's 'little ships' that carried 12,000 hides in 1370 may have been fishing boats. In 1378 the same William, in association with another well-known Bristol merchant, John Barstaple, collected 8,000 again in various 'little ships', but they were afraid to take the same to Calais because of the king's enemies and storms at sea. Smaller boats would be better able to negotiate the harbours and havens of the Atlantic coast, perhaps trading directly with the local Irish.[7]

The Gaelic Irish lords were aware of the commercial value of hides and the O'Malley claimed in right of his chieftaincy to be entitled to take the hides of all the cattle slaughtered within his country. O'Malley's lands were bounded on three sides by the sea and included fine havens in Clew Bay and Killary Harbour. The trade in hides with the Gaelic chiefs is likely to have had connections with a reciprocal trade in fish, wine and cloth. The Anglo-Irish lords were not unaware of this valuable trade either, for a dispute in Drogheda in 1313-14 between Richard de Burgo, earl of Ulster, and customs officials resulted in the exchequer reaffirming that every magnate might send hides from port to port without paying custom.[8]

The weight and bulk of hides made transport overland difficult and, when convenient, people with hides to sell shipped them by sea to the larger ports, where merchants of the staple controlled their sale and export. Agents of Anglo-Irish magnates or of Gaelic lords arriving with cargoes were one source of hides for the merchants of the ports. The merchants themselves also travelled in search of hides. Merchants of Waterford and Ross used small boats on the Suir, Nore and Barrow for bringing hides purchased in parts of Kilkenny and Carlow to these ports. In 1471 John Butler, Genkin Molgan and Nicholas Devereux, citizens of Ross, freighted two boats with 800 hides at Thomastown, Inistioge and St. Mullins, and brought them the 35 miles or so downriver to Waterford for tanning, after which they were sent to Bristol in a ship belonging to Devereux.

Dublin, Waterford and Galway had laws governing trade with the Irish and some regulations regarding the purchase of hides survive in the Waterford municipal records. In 1469-70 it was decreed that no one was to buy fresh hides for more than 10d. a hide or salted hides above 10s. a dicker (10). Prices were again fixed by the municipality in 1485-6 for townspeople buying hides and friezes in the neighbouring counties of Waterford, Kilkenny, Tipperary, Wexford and Carlow. No one was to pay more than 14d. for a fresh

12 *Ireland,* 1339 (redrawn by T.J. Westropp pl. XLII, *R.I.A. Proc.,* XXXI, sect c, 1913)   This drawing omits the compass lines of the original by Angelino Dulcert (see below p. 114). Note the prominence of the Suir, Nore and Barrow river system.

hide or more than 13s. 4d. for a dicker of salted hides. In contrast a Galway regulation of 1515, which aimed at restricting the trade to the city market, stated that no one was to go outside the liberties to buy hides or 'to make bargayn for the same'. These civic regulations refer to trade with outsiders, as freemen among themselves were allowed to buy and sell 'as dere and goode' as they wished in the city.[9]

Throughout the middle ages, hides in one form or another were used to provide shoes, gloves, saddles, harness, bags, belts, rugs and writing materials. In the towns, as the archaeological evidence from medieval Dublin clearly shows, hides provided raw material for a great number of craft workers. Shoemakers are perhaps the most

81

obvious of those whose work depended on hides. John Hamound of Dublin had a large shoemaking business and when he died in 1388 he had several hides and skins in stock plus 116 pairs of shoes. He was owed money by 22 different persons for boots and shoes, one for as many as 30 pairs of shoes, another for 168 pairs.

There are some passing references to hides in family records. An expense account of the earl of Ormond c. 1400 mentions eleven hides bought in Kilkenny for 3s. 11d. and, when Sir Christopher Plunkett of Dunsany died in 1462, he owed Awly O'Doffermoth 2 marks for hides.[10] A very clear indication of the importance of hides in the trade of medieval Ireland occurs in two wills of merchants who were members of the Blake family in Galway. The will of John Oge Blake, who died in 1420, includes among his debtors Thomas Reany, who owed 25 hides in payment for English cloth and 50 in payment for wine. Thadeus O'Mlheyn and Thadeus O'Longayn owed 285 in payment for nine quarters of salt, one dozen (14 x 2 yards) of cloth and two parts of a tun of wine. In the will of John, the son of Henry Blake, dated 1468, it emerges that the hide may have been used as a unit of exchange. He declares that he owes hides to certain merchants some of whom are similarly indebted to him, including one Collas of Bristol and John Byssum, a Breton merchant who owes 40 hides for corn. But John Blake's principal debtors were Irish: Karolus O'Deolleayn, Gillacriste McKenny, Donatus O'Grane, Dermot O'Colgen, Molhony McFlaherty and others, all listed as owing various quantities of hides, presumably for merchandise received from him. The debts owed to Thomas Arthur of Limerick (died 1426) by his Irish customers are listed in pounds, shillings and pence, indicating an interesting difference between the local economies of the two towns, which were on the fringes of English influence in the fifteenth century.[11]

Finally in this context it is worth noting that occasional Breton shipmasters, hired by Irish merchants, were paid partly in money and partly in hides. Paul Bybmaec, who skippered a ship to Dingle in 1500, received of his fee 40 ecus d'or, 10 ecus and 7½ *osaques* of hides.[12]

The great source of all these hides was the huge herds of cattle, which were the most important element of the economy. Particularly in the Gaelic and gaelicised areas cattle were the measure of a chieftain's wealth. Large numbers of people were concerned with the management and care of the herds, which rarely could be housed or stall-fed. Although the evidence is scattered and scant, it seems certain that the great bulk of hides came to the markets from these areas. Apart from some coastal trading by English and foreign mariners, the far-reaching trade in Irish hides in the middle ages was largely dependent on extensive interchanges between the merchants of the towns, particularly the port towns, and the native Irish.

13　*Western Europe, showing ports trading with Ireland.*

83

III

Minerals and Stone

SALT AND IRON FROM BRITTANY AND SPAIN

The salt trade Salt and iron were, with wine, the necessities that Ireland lacked and so they figure prominently in trade throughout the middle ages. English and foreign merchants coming to buy merchandise in Ireland regularly brought with them salt and iron, sure of profitable sales. Merchants from the Irish ports frequently negotiated cargoes of salt and iron in England and on the Continent that were to be carried home in their own vessels or in chartered ships. Very importantly Ireland in her import needs was favoured by the geographical coincidence that conveniently placed the principal western European sources of salt, iron and wine together on the shores of the Bay of Biscay. This meant that enterprising merchants trading in various commodities could organise a 'round trip'.

One great source of salt in the middle ages was Bourgneuf Bay, known then as The Bay, which was situated a few miles south of the Loire estuary between Brittany and Poitou. Here vast quantities of salt were extracted from seawater, by evaporation in artifically constructed salt pans in the shallow sea. This salt was shipped all over Europe and particularly to the Hanseatic fishing stations. England, however, supplied most of her own needs employing the same method along her low-lying coast.[1]

The Bay was convenient to Brittany, which had established trading connections with Ireland by the beginning of the fourteenth century. An enquiry conducted in 1309-10 mentions that a Drogheda merchant, Ralph Kenefeg, frequently bought salt there in exchange for horses. Not all Bretons were peaceful merchants, however, and piracy was endemic off the coast of their homeland. The most frequent victims were ships laden with salt and wine bound for England and Ireland. Compensation for those robbed took the form usual in maritime law and frequently backed by royal authority, namely, the

84

arrest of any Breton merchants with their ships and goods until satisfaction was obtained. In 1387 an order was issued for the arrest of Bretons coming to Ireland to compensate a merchant of Winchelsea, whose cargo of salt was stolen as he sailed home from The Bay. In 1412, in similar action against piracy, three Breton vessels laden with salt worth 700 marks were seized at Dalkey by John Penkeston of Dublin, who had letters of reprisals granted against Bretons by the king's lieutenant in Ireland.

Probably to guard against such happenings, with the increase of trade between Brittany, Dublin and Drogheda in the fifteenth century, Breton merchants coming to Ireland with salt and iron secured special safe conducts. When Breton shipmasters returned home, they frequently carried Irish corn with them. Ynoni Caurce, the master of the *Juliana* of Garrande, brought twelve weys of wheat 'to the parts of Bay' in 1432.[2]

The import of salt and iron was a vital section of the trade of the Irish ports, particularly those of the east coast in medieval times. These goods frequently came in large ships which, like some of the wine ships, were unable to berth at the quaysides of Drogheda and Dublin. Instead these vessels anchored at Dalkey, Lambay and Howth, and Irish merchants received special permission to travel out and buy wine, iron and salt, for according to the regulations of the statute of the Staple severe penalties could be incurred for trading outside the city area. In 1364 the merchants of Drogheda complained when forced to conduct all their foreign trade through the staple of Calais. There, they declared 'wine, iron, salt or other merchandise suitable for Ireland' could not be found. Accordingly they were licensed to trade directly with England, Gascony and elsewhere, as was their custom.[3]

English merchants participated in the Irish salt trade. Salt was landed at Crook in Waterford harbour *c.* 1320 by a merchant of the Cinque Ports on a voyage to Ross. Thomas de Byndon, a leading merchant of Southampton, contracted in 1337 with some Galway merchants to supply 1,000 quarters of salt and his ship, the *Gracedieu*, was on its way when arrested near Waterford for military service. Walter Frompton, several times mayor of Bristol, also freighted salt to Ireland, as did his fellow townsmen John Mitford, William Cotom and William Knap in 1377 and 1397.

Some large-scale salt and iron imports are recorded in the fifteenth century in connection with Dublin and Drogheda. In 1431 certain Italian and Aragonese merchants living in London, loaded a Venetian carrack with salt and iron at Gerand in Brittany. They were sailing to Dublin when the ship was seized and the cargo disposed of in Plymouth.[4] John Gayncote, a merchant of Dartmouth, combined with a group of Drogheda merchants in 1435 in what must have been a very ambitious undertaking. They secured a permit to bring from Brittany eight 200-ton ships, each crewed by up to 40 men, with cargoes of salt, iron and other goods. That same year another permit was issued to two members of this group to bring from Brittany two ships of similar size and cargo. One reason behind such a large undertaking was that Drogheda and the east coast ports appear to have been depending on imports of salt direct from The Bay, as shipments from Chester dwindled towards the middle of the fifteenth century.

Similar reasons to those which made The Bay attractive to merchants seeking salt drew them to Spain. On its south-western coast low sand dunes broken by lagoons lent themselves to the production of salt from sea-water. The availability of salt, along with the wines from Lisbon and Cadiz and iron from the Cantabrian mountains, resulted in profitable voyages to procure goods that were always in demand both in England and in Ireland.

Although there is evidence to suggest that Irish merchants traded with Spain in the early fourteenth century — Robert Russell got a safe conduct to bring wines, large salt and other merchandise from there to his home port of Ross in 1315-16 — the full development of the Spanish-Irish trade took place after the mid-fifteenth century. At this time England was losing control of Gascony and looking more to Spain for supplies of wine, salt and luxury goods, much of which came through Bristol.[5]

Ireland's close trading links with Bristol meant that quantities of Spanish iron and salt as well as wine reached the Irish ports through Bristol merchants. In 1434 David Selly of London and Walter Power, an ironmonger of Bristol, arranged to bring a ship of 200 tons laden with salt, iron and other goods from Spain to Ireland. But the pattern of trade between Bristol, Spain and Ireland is probably better exemplified in the voyage of the *Julian* of Bristol in 1453. This ship carried English products to Spain, then proceeded directly to Galway and Sligo with wine, salt and honey, and returned to Bristol with hides and other Irish produce.

Spanish ships came to Bristol with large cargoes of iron and salt according to the evidence of the customs accounts, and the same sources indicate that small quantities were re-exported to Ireland. Salt from The Bay also came to Ireland via Bristol. On 19 October 1497 the *Sebastian* of Vannes arrived in Bristol from Brittany with

THE OVERSEAS TRADE
OF DROGHEDA
XIII – XV cents

● 13th CENT
● 14th CENT
● 15th CENT

ICELAND 1458

AYR

ON
CARLISLE

DROGHEDA

CHESTER

TENBY

CARDIFF BRISTOL

LONDON

SOUTHAMPTON

CALAIS

DIEPPE

BRITTANY

LA ROCHELLE

BORDEAUX

GDANSK
1384

LEYDEN

LISBON 1480

SPAIN 1354

14

fifty tuns of salt and sailed for Ireland four days later with twenty eight tuns and some cloth. The bulk of Irish salt imports in the fifteenth century came directly from Brittany and Spain and some permits, like that issued to Thomas Skethe of Dublin in 1435, licensed the merchant to bring salt from either country. As is the case with most medieval trading voyages, the factors of war and weather determined the port of lading as much as market costs.[6]

A severe shortage of salt merited a report in the Annals of Ulster in 1486 and the chronicler remarked that jesting folk were composing its elegy. Imported salt was used in connection with the fishing industry and for the processing of hides of the great cattle herds of the countryside. Its value and importance are indicated by the number of surviving wills of the medieval period that mention amounts of salt large and small. John Mold of Malahide was a small-time farmer and fisherman. In his will, dated 1474, he left 40s. worth of corn, 10 sheep, 4 pigs and a foal, 10 barrels of herrings, 3 nets and 4 crannocks* of salt valued at 16s.[7]

Salt was essential for preserving meat in the days before refrigeration. Owing to the shortage of winter feed, thousands of cattle were slaughtered each autumn and much of this meat was salted. The important towns had a meat store that was kept stocked by the municipality. In 1402-3 some burgesses of Drogheda received a permit to take a ship to Ulster to buy beeves and cattle for the 'larddre' or meat store of the town. They brought with them old wine, and one and a half weys of salt for preserving the meat.[8]

In Waterford (1485-6) the butchers were responsible for supplies of meat in the city and were permitted to buy live cattle in the surrounding countryside. They were paid 2d. for each cow killed and cut up for the larder of the city. Salted meat was an important item in military supplies and 'bacons' were requisitioned occasionally for the army. Although exports of salted meat on a commercial basis were rare in medieval Ireland, a considerable trade in salted beef developed in the sixteenth century, some of which was exported to England through the ports and more was used in trade between visiting Spanish fishermen and local Gaelic chiefs.[9]

The sale of salt was subject to municipal regulations similar to those governing the sale of wine. The town officials of Drogheda tried to prevent a Genoese merchant, Lukyn Spinola, from selling his ship-load of salt 'save in gross', but he successfully contested the legality of the prohibition. Waterford Corporation, however, passed

*Weights and measures varied according to commodities: 5 crannocks of salt = 1 ton.

15 *Timber-framed house, Dublin* (*R.S.A.I. Jn.*, XL, 1890-1) This
house stood in Castle St., Dublin before its demolition in 1813.

a law in 1433-4 which stated that no man could sell salt 'out of ship',
but only from his cellar. Regulations such as these were aimed at
securing a monopoly of all retail trading for the guild of merchants.
At the same time they ensured that in practice foreign merchants
could sell only to members of the guilds.

Salt merchants appear to have been no different from the average
merchant retailer of the Irish port towns. These rarely confined their
business to one commodity, nor does their wealth appear to have
been completely tied up in trade. Robert de Moenes, a citizen of
Dublin in 1326, owned a cloth shop as well as a salt depot, but besides
these he had income from properties leased out in various parts of

the city. Peter Higley, also of Dublin, appears to have concentrated his city business in the retail of salt and iron. His stocks in 1476 were £32 worth of salt and £9 6s. 8d. worth of iron and, according to his account book, he was owed £57 by various customers. He, too, owned houses in the city, but in addition he invested part of his capital in 40 acres of land which he rented in Killeek in north Co. Dublin. There he had about 20 cattle, 50 sheep and 9 acres under tillage. He also had 7 cart-horses and a number of wagons, presumably in connection with his business in the city, since the prices charged by the regular carters were very high, particularly for salt and iron.[10]

The people of the countryside needed salt not only for preserving food but also for making butter and cheese, and their supplies were obtained through the towns and local markets. Part of the obligations of the tenants of the manor of Moyaliff in Co. Tipperary was to carry salt and iron from Cashel, whenever the baliff required it. The will of John Oge Blake of Galway (1420) shows that he traded in salt with Gaelic families and with the de Burgo lords.[11]

The iron trade Iron came to Ireland almost always with cargoes of salt in great ships from Brittany and Spain. This indispensable commodity came usually in the form of bars or 'peyces of iron' and was the raw material from which smiths and other craftsmen fashioned tools, farm implements, weapons, horseshoes, nails and a great variety of other articles. Numerous entries in the *Account Roll of Holy Trinity* (1337-46) refer to the purchase of iron and to the manufacture or repair of a multitude of objects, including buckets, chains, window bars, locks and keys. The building and maintenance of castles, houses and ships all required large quantities of iron. Some raw iron came to Ireland from English ports and in 1355, when the export of iron from England to any country was forbidden, an exception was made of Ireland.[12]

Manufactured iron goods were imported from Chester, which supplied, in particular, cutlery and arrows. Most frequently mentioned among manufactured metal imports is hammered metal-ware called 'battery', which included all varieties of pots and pans. One consignment of 316 cauldrons was seized in 1395 for non-payment of customs and given to Janico Dartas. In the Bristol customs account many cargoes coming to Ireland included battery.

Archaeological evidence points to considerable imports of pottery, especially glazed jugs from south-eastern England, but these items were duty free and do not appear in the accounts. There is an isolated instance in the 1492-3 account of Flemish jugs valued at 12s. being imported from Ireland to Bristol.[13]

Metal pots and utensils were considered items of exceptional value and figure prominently in wills. In a parish or village there was, no doubt, much lending and borrowing of the bigger vessels. In 1476 Nicholas Delaber bequeathed his largest pot and skillet to be held for common use among his neighbours, rich and poor, in Balrothery, Co. Dublin, and in 1472 Joan White willed her three-legged pan and a trough to the villagers of Leixlip, 'for the health of my soul and the souls of my ancestors'. Pieces of armour were also valued possessions and were passed on from father to son. Robert de Moenes mentioned above, had 'the makings' of two suits of armour which he left between his sons and relations. The citizens were frequently called on to defend their walled towns or to send a contingent to join the lord deputy's army if fighting nearby. Various forces of Dubliners joined in campaigns against 'Irish rebels' including the O'Byrnes and O'Moores in the fifteenth century.[14]

Waterford burgesses were obliged to have arms and armour — at least a coat of mail, a helmet and a hand weapon. The city throughout the middle ages was so often under attack that in 1446 it was granted what amounted to a licence to make private war: 'to march out with banners flying . . . against the Poers from whom they have suffered . . .', and graphic accounts survive of the brief but bloody encounters that took place. The native Irish were always seeking arms and armour, but merchants were expressly forbidden ever to sell arms to them.[15]

In 1393 the royal council ordered, under penalty of £1,000, the arrest of a ship in Drogheda which merchants had loaded with wine, victuals and artillery (*artillerie*) to 'aid and comfort the Irish enemies of the king'. In the increasing number of licences to trade with the Irish granted in the fifteenth century this precept was reiterated. Waterford Corporation forbade the sale of iron to the Irish to prevent them from constructing boats. Later, in 1481, the same body banned the sale of crossbows, 'gonnes small nor greate nether gonnpouder' to anyone outside the city. Significantly the regulation adds 'without licence of Maire and Counsaile for tyme beyng', for despite severe penalties and obvious danger to themselves, profit was the prime consideration of the medieval merchants. The Irish got their weapons sometimes through the towns, but they also had a major source of iron goods, salt, cloth and arms in foreign fishermen, who came in increasing numbers in pursuit of the herring and who paid in kind for fishing and landing rights.[16]

Quality millstones were of great importance in the production of good flour, free from grit. The best millstone quarries in Britain were situated near Penmon, on Anglesey. From there millstones were exported as far as the Baltic states. Both large millstones and smaller hand-grindstones were shipped to Ireland in the later middle ages and Welsh millstones are mentioned in the murage customs of Dublin.

Top-class stones were also quarried in France, and Andernach in the Rhine valley was a noted source of millstones. French millstones were used in medieval Ireland: the three stones confiscated from the Frescobaldi in 1304 may have been brought from France for sale here. A description of the King's Mills near Dublin Castle in 1306, mentions an old French millstone and an old English one. Repairs to the castle mills in 1313-14 necessitated the expenditure of 28s. 9d. on a Welsh grindstone. This figure included the cost of the stone, the carriage and dressing of the stone before it was fixed into place. When the royal mills at Leixlip were repaired c. 1330, two French millstones (*molaribus Gallicanis*) were purchased for £7 6s. 8d. and transported to Leixlip at a cost of 6s. 8d. In view of the fact that it cost 6s. 8d. to transport the stones fifteen miles from Dublin to Leixlip, a large proportion of the overall price must have been for shipment from the French quarries.[1] Unloading the stones at Dublin meant the use of the great crane on the quay. A directive was issued in 1467-8 by the municipality ordering those who owned the millstones cluttering the pavement around the crane to shift them or face a fine of 3s. 4d.[2]

Significant quantities of the building stone known as Dundry oolite were imported in the thirteenth and fourteenth centuries. A recent survey shows the presence of Dundry stone in some thirty-eight buildings, mainly in south-eastern Ireland. Most of these are ecclesiastical buildings, but some castles are included in the survey. All the buildings with Dundry stone are located in the ports of Drogheda, Dublin, Ross, Cork and Wexford or in places situated on the greater rivers, such as the Suir (Athassel) and the Nore (Inistioge, Thomastown and Kilkenny). This trade in stone is further evidence of the significant contact between Bristol and south-eastern Ireland. It also emphasises the importance of water-borne transport for moving heavy materials. Waterman hints that certain tomb effigies at Ross and Athassel (Co. Tipperary) may have been brought ready-made from Somerset. Similarly there may have been some import of carved alabasters from Bristol in the later middle ages.[3]

Other building materials imported into Ireland included lead and a considerable trade developed in the shipment of slates from the northern Welsh ports to Ireland. In 1286-7 the sum of 60s. was paid for one wagon-load and ten stones of lead brought from Wales 'for roofing the castle of the Island' (Great Island, Waterford Harbour, near Dunbrody Abbey.)

In connection with king's works, notably the maintenance and repair of castles, normal commercial activity was altered when supplies, transport and tradesmen were requisitioned by royal officials. The surviving records of the central administration have numerous instances of this unpopular procedure. The following is a typical example: Repairs were needed to Dublin Castle in 1399 with the result that John Inglewood and William Blythe were appointed to provide stones, timber, tiles, lead and nails, and to take and arrest carpenters, masons, plumbers and transport, in England, Wales and Ireland, within the liberties as well as without (Church lands excepted). They were to bring to Ireland two carpenters, two masons, and two plumbers 'discreet, sufficient and approved' and place them on the said work. The necessary ships and mariners were to be arrested also and 'all for the king's money reasonably to be paid'.[4]

IV

Luxury Imports and Miscellaneous Exports

Silks and fine metalwork   In addition to the fine quality scarlet cloth mentioned above, small consignments of which occasionally reached Ireland, there was some import of silk and silken garments. It is unlikely that England was the main supplier of silk, since the amounts in the Bristol customs accounts are very small. In 1480 only a few pounds came through that port, worth £3, but this increased to 98 lbs in 1492-3 and reached 243 lbs worth £162 in 1504-5. One of the principal uses of silk was in the making of ecclesiastical vestments and civic insignia. An account in the pipe roll of 1341-2 noted that the keeper of the stores at Dublin Castle bought silk, cendal (?Kendal green cloth), linen cloth and other necessities for two standards bearing the king's arms, and two pairs of vestments for use in the royal chapels in the castle and in the exchequer. Another entry relating to the purchase of special cloth occurred in the pipe roll of 1332-3. This was for payment to a Drogheda merchant 'for a cloth of divers colours bought for the king's use to cover both exchequers of the king at Dublin and for clipping, cutting and sewing the same.

The inventory of the possessions of Archbishop Walton includes a long list of fine cloths and vestments, some of which he brought with him from England on his appointment to the see of Dublin in 1472. There is mention of vestments of green damask, a coverlet of blue serge, a quilt embroidered with eagles in the middle, and a coverlet of tapestry with an eagle and the letters J and V set therein.[1]

In earlier centuries the Italian merchants most likely shared in the trade in costly cloth, vestments and church ornaments. When Stephen de Fulbourn died as archbishop of Tuam in 1288, he owned 'a

94

chasuble of red samite, a great cross of pearls, two precious embroidered choir-copes, a clasp for a cope with an image of the Diety and precious stones ...'. In Waterford there is a fine set of four Benediction copes and a set of High Mass vestments of brocaded velvet on cloth of gold, with designs in red and green silk. Catriona McLeod suggests that the workmanship is characteristic of late fifteenth-century Italian and Flemish workshops and adds that the vestments may have been a gift of Henry VII to the city. Henry VII presented vestments to certain churches in England. He rewarded Waterford's loyalty to him in the grant of a new charter in 1488 and of the motto *urbs intacta manet Waterfordia* (Waterford remains a loyal city) in 1497.

John Collyn, dean of Holy Trinity, Waterford, from 1441 was a wealthy cleric who founded the chantry of St. Saviour's in that city. He bequeathed to the cathedral many liturgical, devotional and legal books, vestments, and valuable plate including a censer or thurible of 41 ozs. of silver that had six little statues around the top. Details from medieval Irish wills and inventories and the existence of fine craftsmanship of Irish provenance such as the beautiful crozier and mitre commissioned in 1418 for Conor O'Dea, bishop of Limerick and the processional cross of Lislaughtin (near Ballylongford, Co. Kerry) indicate that metalwork of contemporary international design was produced in the workshops of the towns and of the ports in particular.

There is some evidence for imports (John Collyn, for example, mentions that he had his seal made in London), but it is equally certain that gold- and silversmiths of high standing were working in medieval Ireland. Thomas O'Carryd who made the O'Dea mitre, was presumably a Limerick artist. Some Irish goldsmiths, such as the colourful mint-master Germanus Lynch (*fl.* 1441-83) and his apprentice Patrick Keyne, were trained in London. Others enjoyed the high status of *sair* or *ollamh* in Gaelic Ireland and the death in 1471 of Mathew Ó Mailruanaigh *ollamh* in metalwork (*cerda*) to Mag Uidhir (Maguire) is recorded in the Annals of Ulster. In 1462 a goldsmith in Trim repaired a chalice for Sir Christopher Plunkett, and Archbishop Tregury of Dublin ran into problems of territorial jurisdiction when bringing his processional cross for repair to Drogheda in 1451.

Goldsmithing was one craft, along with medicine, which seems to have bridged the ethnic barriers in medieval Ireland and some Gaelic Irish craftsmen settled in the towns. One Dermot Lynchy, goldsmith, was admitted to the franchise of Dublin in 1473 and Donal

Oge O'Vollaghan, also a goldsmith, was made a freeman of Galway in 1500.[3]

Honey, spices and luxury foods Honey as a sweetening agent was imported to supplement local supplies. Along with spices such as saffron and aniseed, small quantities figure frequently in Bristol's exports to Ireland. A quantity of honey being shipped from Bristol to Limerick in 1401 was seized from a vessel sheltering in Dingle. In 1449-50, Limerick was receiving honey and other provisions under contract from a Breton merchant, Maurice de la Noe.[4]

Spices were used in cooking in wealthy households and were a small but valuable import throughout the middle ages. The *Nicholas* of Downpatrick (Co. Down), which was wrecked off Portmarnock in 1306, was carrying a varied cargo of wine, wax, pots, coffers of jewels and several barrels of spices. Many different spices were used in the kitchens of Holy Trinity Priory, Dublin, including pepper that cost 20d. a pound while pepper was among the earl of Ormond's purchases in Kilkenny *c.* 1400. That the native Irish lords ate spiced foods is clear from references in literary works and from descriptions of feasts and banquets. A charming little story (probably sixteenth century) illustrates the point. O'Grady sent one of his followers to the town of Cashel for spice, that is, for pepper and aniseed. The boy was told to memorise the words well and he started to repeat them over and over. Coming near the town he fell and was unconscious for a while. When he came to himself, the first words he uttered were *piopar agus ainis* (pepper and aniseed).[5]

Almonds were popular as desserts or sweets. When Henry II came to Ireland in 1171, he brought spices and cordials for medicinal use, along with 569 lbs of almonds. Joan de Botiller (Butler) ran up considerable debts with the Ricardi in 1287, including expenditure on furs and cloth, typical of a rich man's wife in any age. Among the lesser items that she bought were spices (8s. 10d.) and figs and raisins (23s. 4d.). In Holy Trinity Priory almonds were sometimes served with rice, and figs were on the menu when Sir Thomas Wogan and other distinguished guests came to dine on 23 January 1338. Four pounds of almonds cost 6d. in Kilkenny *c.* 1400. Two amphorae containing kernels of almonds were discovered in Cork in 1928, and were most likely lost accidentally from a ship in medieval times.[6]

There is scant evidence for the import of citrus fruit. Only once is fruit mentioned in the Holy Trinity accounts; pears were served to the archbishop — but these may well have been homegrown. It

16 *Monks singing* (*Facs. nat. Mss Ire.* IV, 4) Illustration from a
   manuscript made before 1368 for the Cathedral of Holy Trinity,
   Dublin now in the Bodleian Library, Oxford.

seems likely that fruit and olive oil were sometimes carried by the
wine ships that came to Ireland from the Continent. Bristol merchants
in the fifteenth century imported fruit and oil from the Iberian
peninsula, but re-exports to Ireland are insignificant in the customs
accounts.

One Bristol ship, loaded at Lisbon with thirty tuns of wine, two
pipes of oil, 500 lbs of wax and twenty-six 'couples' of fruit to bring
'to the city of Dublin or to England', was arrested at Kinsale, whither
it was driven by a storm. High-quality wax, used for sealing documents
and for candles, was occasionally imported — Henry II brought over
1,000 lbs in 1171. There was some export trade to Bristol in
unspecified wax and in tallow, the latter as a by-product of the trade
in cattle hides.[7]

Skins and furs Sheep, lambs and the wild animals of the woods and mountains of Ireland were the basis of a profitable trade in skins and furs throughout the medieval period. Most highly prized were the marten skins that were used in decorating and lining the robes of the wealthy. It is noted in Domesday Book that Chester paid part of her royal dues in marten skins, which may point to a trade at that time in both Welsh and Irish marten skins. King Philip Augustus, in his charter to Rouen of 1207, declared that a *tymbre* (said to equal forty skins) of Irish marten skins should be furnished by every boat coming from Ireland. If the merchants swore that no skins were available at their port of lading in Ireland, they were allowed to pay £10 instead. A similar tax is mentioned in 1242, also in connection with a grant to Rouen.[8]

Irish fox and lambskins, particularly black lambskins, as well as marten skins, are mentioned in the wardrobe accounts of some of the English kings. In 1396 Richard II appointed John Scot to buy in Ireland as many skins and furs called 'wildeware' as were needed for the expenses of the royal wardrobe. Perhaps it was on account of their scarcity and value that marten skins were specifically excluded from a trading permit issued to Ross in 1409. In 1415 Henry V assigned John Baxter, William Balfe and the aptly named William del Warderobe to 'seize, purchase and arrest' whatever skins of martens, *mappekins* (?), rabbits, otters and squirrels they required. One suspects that here the royal power was being used to ensure that the court would not be short of a luxury commodity such as skins. Similar thinking appears to be behind the ban on the sale and export of hawks and falcons.

The frequent wars of fifteenth-century Ireland do not seem to have diminished the country's reputation as a supplier of skins to England. To quote the anonymous author of *The Libelle of Englyshe Polycye*, c. 1436-8:

> And marterns gode bene in here marchaundye;
> Hertys hydes and other hydes of venerye,
> Skynnes of oter, squerel, and Irysh hare,
> Of shepe, lambe and fox is here chaffare,
> Felles of kydde and conyes grete plente.[9]

Some prominent London skin merchants such as William Pountfreyt, who had attorneys in Ireland, shipped skins directly to London, but the bulk of Irish skins and furs went to England through Bristol and Chester. E.M. Veale suggested that skins arriving from Ireland were undressed and that the processing was done either in the port of arrival or, in the case of skins imported through Chester, in Coventry. In this connection she referred to records of the Skinners' Company that suggest frequent contact between the citizens of Bristol, Chester and Coventry and the skinners of London. The wills of two Coventry merchants who died in Dublin in the second half of the fifteenth century imply that both had interests in the skin trade, and mention quantities of lambskins, goatskins and sheepskins. In the early fifteenth century between 16,500 and 48,000 sheepskins and lambskins worth from £70 to £150 per annum are recorded in the Bristol customs accounts. The lighter skins of the smaller animals numbered 13,252 (worth £56 10s. 7d.) in 1403-4 and 14,877 in 1437-8. Later the annual import declined to average only about 500 skins, until in the early sixteenth century the general upsurge in trade with Bristol brought about a slight increase.[10]

Timber   Timber in the middle ages was an indispensable commodity in the economy of every country and Ireland at that time was well endowed with forests and woods. It has been estimated that about fifteen per cent of the country was wooded *c.* 1300. The river valleys of Leinster and Munster were among the most densely wooded regions and provided a convenient source of timber both for building purposes and for fuel in the port towns.

Part of the indenture (1370) between William of Windsor and John McKenemargho, 'captain of his nation', stated that he would permit the citizens of Limerick to cut down his woods in Thomond for the repair of the city, and timber to be cut in the woods and carried to the city for sale. Firewood frequently arrived at the towns by river. Objectors to a new weir built on the Liffey at Lucan in 1306 mentioned that it hindered the passage of boats taking firewood to Dublin. New Ross received firewood by boat and when the earl of Ormond as chief governor, planned to spend Christmas 1393 there with his retinue, great amounts of food and drink were requisitioned and ten boat-loads of firewood.

The trade in firewood was largely managed by native Irishmen. The civil regulations of Waterford imply that 'wode bote men' were sometimes troublesome. The municipality passed a law in 1458-9 that all foreigners and servants dwelling within the city and suburbs had to take an oath to be true to the king and the city of Waterford, 'and in especial those that bene maistres of wod botes and botemen'. In 1508-9 the city re-enacted restrictions on the transport of wood and it seems that at that time a regular source of supply was The Rower, about 10 miles up the Barrow estuary from Waterford.[11]

Firewood was vital for heating and cooking, but turf (peat) was also burned. The cutting and harvesting of turf are sometimes listed among the duties of manorial tenants. Its use in towns probably depended on the proximity of bogs but, apart from requiring less labour in production than wood, as firing it was also relatively safer to use since it burnt without sparks. This was an important consideration in crowded medieval towns with many wooden and thatched houses where fire was a fearful hazard. Waterford and Dublin had many laws to combat this danger, the former city going so far as to ban all thatched roofs in 1388.

To ensure supplies of firing must have been an important consideration in relationships between local lords and the townspeople. The mayor of Drogheda in 1401-2 had to go as far as Carlingford Lough to buy fuel (*focali*). Some coal was burned, but it is not clear where it came from. Stone-coal was included in a cargo of provisions shipped to Carrickfergus in 1319 and the arrest of a coal vessel is recorded in Dublin in 1322-3.

Wood was bought for fencing and archaeologists have shown that houses made of wattle and daub were common in medieval Irish towns. A very detailed account of the provision of wood for making hurdles in Dublin (1303-4) is related by J.F. Lydon. The hurdles were needed for refitting a fleet of requisitioned ships to take an army with a large number of warhorses to Scotland. Also in Dublin, Holy Trinity Priory bought wood from the local Irish, though the community had some woodland at Clonkeen in the foothills of the mountains. About 1340 payment is recorded for the wages of two men cutting underwood, at 1d. a day, while two more were paid 4d. 'for two nights' watching on the top of the hills through fear of the Irish'.[12]

There was some export of Irish timber, and the sources imply that there was a small but steady trade with England and Wales in the thirteenth century. Irish oak in particular had been sought by the builders of many English churches: in 1224 William of Dublin brought timber for the fabric of Salisbury Cathedral. In medieval France, Irish oak was considered to be especially suitable for furniture and sculpture. The choir-stalls of Rouen Cathedral were carved from Irish oak in 1465-9.

England came to depend more and more on imported timber owing to rapid deforestation in the thirteenth and fourteenth centuries. Most of this timber, which was needed for house construction and

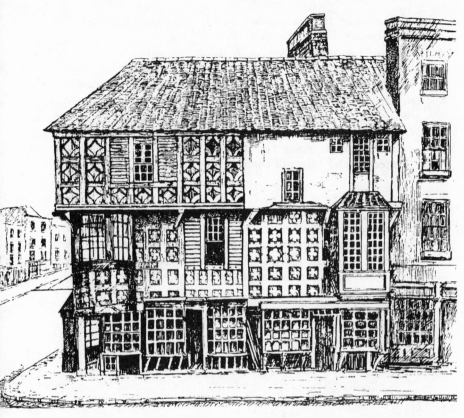

17 *Timber-framed house, Drogheda* (*R.S.A.I. Jn.*, XL, 1890-1) The
house of Nicholas Bathe, built in 1570. It stood in Shop St.,
Drogheda until its demolition in 1825.

shipbuilding, came from Norway and the Baltic countries in Hanseatic
ships, but Ireland too supplied timber, chiefly in the form of sawn
planks or 'boards' as they were called. A list of customs to be collected
at Ipswich *c.* 1300 specified 4d on every hundred of 'borde of Irlond'.
The entry implies that this material was used in house construction
for eaving and wainscotting. In connection with Edward I's campaign
in Wales in 1256, prefabricated wooden assault towers were shipped
from Dublin, Drogheda and Dungarvan. 'Shipboards' from Ireland
figure in several ships' cargoes listed in the Bristol customs accounts.
Boards for planking and scaffolding were also sent to Wales in the
later middle ages. In the account for the repairs to the king's mills

in Pembroke and Carmarthen in 1481-2, payment is recorded for Irish boards.[13]

It would appear, however, that the export of sawn planks was but one segment of the timber trade. Construction and shipbuilding would have been another. As far as trade was concerned, the manufacture of barrels and casks must have been most important. Practically all of the corn, fish and tanned hides exported from the Irish ports in the middle ages was packed in casks and barrels. Unfortunately no details of this aspect of the Irish timber trade are available for the fourteenth and fifteenth centuries.[14]

Birds of prey Hunting with hawks, falcons and other birds of prey was a favourite sport of the medieval nobility. Hawks were valued and treasured, and the pictorial evidence of miniatures and tapestries points to the pride taken in these hunting birds, a pride analogous to that shown by the owners of fine race-horses today. Although very

18 *A king with a falcon (Facs. nat. Mss Ire.,* IV, 4) This drawing meant to represent King John is reduced from the Waterford charter roll, *c.* 1400.

clearly a luxury commodity comparable with the marten skins, Irish hawks and falcons fetched high prices in continental Europe and in England, and attracted the interest of merchants in the later middle ages. Sometimes the volume of exports led to a scarcity of hawks in Ireland. This affected the Anglo-Irish and English upper classes and legislation restricting or banning exports quickly followed.

In 1358 Edward III sent his falconer, William of Troyes, to Ireland to purchase six goshawks and six tercels (male hawks). The treasury of Ireland was ordered to pay for the cost of the birds and for the expenses of the falconer and his varlets. William of Windsor, in the year that he returned to England after his difficult period as chief governor (1376), bought twelve goshawks in Ireland. The export of hawks from Drogheda was forbidden in 1386-7 and in 1389 Richard II ordered that no one was to buy any hawks, falcons or tercels in Ireland, in order to sell them in Ireland, England or elsewhere, on pain of forfeiture or imprisonment.

Such a ban must have been impossible to enforce, although officials were appointed to investigate any breaches of the law. This law appears to have been directed towards a supply of birds for the royal falconries, for in 1394 Richard appointed William Castell to buy falcons and goshawks in Ireland for the king's use 'before all others'. In 1400 Henry IV appointed Hugh Shirley to supervise the purchase of falcons for the king's use in Ireland. Another ban on the buying and selling of such birds was issued in 1403, but John Buxton was appointed to buy falcons in Ireland for the king that same year.[15]

Throughout the fifteenth century the export of falcons continued as a minor but lucrative Irish practice. It is not surprising to note that Bristol merchants were associated with the trade. Nicholas Palmer, a merchant of Bristol, bought a goshawk for the earl of Warwick in the Drogheda area in 1470. The Bristol customs accounts for 1480 record that Morris Crynam brought four hawks from Ireland on a ship of Cork. In the same year heavy tariffs were imposed on hawks for export. The merchants had to pay 13s. 4d. for each goshawk 6s. 8d. for a tercel and 10s. for each falcon exported. The reason given for these duties was that merchants of England and Ireland had taken so many hawks out of the land 'rather for merchandise to be sold than for any other reason ... that no hawks can be found for the pleasure of the king and his lords'. Despite the tariffs, the exports continued and became the subject of further legislation in the reign of Henry VIII, when licences were required for the export of hawks to any country except England.[16]

Horses Considering the importance of horses in the whole economy of the middle ages, it is surprising that so few references to the buying and selling of them have survived. There were different types of horses. An inquisition of 1284 distinguished between 'great horses, palfreys and other horses'. An inventory of the goods of the Templars confiscated in Crook, Co. Waterford, in 1330-1 mentions *affri* valued at 4s. 6d. each, wagon horses at 6s. 8d., a *sumpter* or baggage horse worth 30s., and a horse 'which was in a stable' worth 40s. An *afer* was a poor breed of horse used in farm work, although on the demesnes the heavy work and ploughing were done by oxen. Earlier in the same roll there was a list of horses bought in various parts of Ireland and shipped for service in the Scottish war in 1319. The list gave details of the colours and prices and even included the pet-name of each horse! J.F. Lydon points out that the hobelar, or light-mounted cavalryman, was a significant Irish contribution to medieval warfare. They made their first appearance outside Ireland in the Scottish wars, fighting with Edward I.[17]

The great warhorses used by the nobles and military commanders were treasured animals. In Dublin after the Bruce invasion, John Fitzthomas was allowed £10 for his warhorse allegedly worth £20 when killed in the war with the Scots, and Robert Bagot was awarded £20 for another warhorse purchased by him for the king's use.

In the 1320s the earl of Kildare had three studs at Kildare with 9 stallions, 184 mares and 64 foals, all managed by Irish stud-keepers. In 1310 George de Rupe and the sheriff of Waterford were commissioned by the treasurer to locate and hold for the king the stud that belonged to John de Bovenill deceased which certain Co. Waterford men had driven from Carlow.

The Gaelic Irish chiefs kept studs also. When the Catalan Raymond viscount of Perelhos, visited Niall Mór O'Neill while on pilgrimage to St. Patrick's Purgatory, Lough Derg in 1397, he estimated that O'Neill had 3,000 horses! At this time Art Mór MacMurchada had a horse that cost him 400 cows and travelled at a speed that amazed the followers of Richard II. Perhaps it is the white one that Art is shown riding in the miniature.[18]

In the normal commercial export of horses a great number seem to have been sent to Brittany, especially from Dublin and Drogheda. Trading between these ports and Brittany was well developed by the fifteenth century, but seems to have begun in the early fourteenth in connection with the import of salt. In an inquiry into the activities of a Drogheda merchant, Ralph Kenfeg, conducted in 1309-10, it is mentioned that at various times he bought salt at a place called

19 *Art Mac Murchadha meeting the earl of Gloucester*, 1399 (*Archaeologia* XX, 1824)   The Irish king is shown riding barefoot and bareback to meet the heavily armoured troops of Richard II. The original illustration is a coloured miniature in Jean Creton's chronicle (British Library, MS Harleian 1319), a contemporary account of Richard II's Irish expedition.

St. John de Naungle in exchange for horses. In 1358 Richard Hegrene of Dublin sailed to England with 200 crannocks of corn and six horses for Brittany.

In 1409 Simon Wykyn, merchant, was permitted to export six horses. A group of Drogheda merchants *c.* 1446 were travelling to Brittany with thirty-four horses and a cargo of hides, then they put into Dartmouth in a storm and had their horses taken. In 1451 two Drogheda merchants got a licence to sell horses (and other goods) to Bretons and Scots for five years and the following year John Caunton of Dublin was permitted to take four horses to Britanny or Spain. Irish horses, 'Gentyll horsys that be callyd hobbeys', were evidently well known in Europe at this time, for one Irish hackney (*haulbin d'Irlande*) was considered to be a suitable gift for an important official in Normandy, and in 1471 Francisco Salvatico, writing to Galeazzo Maria Sforza, duke of Milan, said: 'I am all ready to go and also to proceed to Ireland, whence all the hackney horses come'.[19]

Irish horses went also to England. The prior of Bath loaded six horses and various provisions at Waterford in 1374, 'to sell and make his profit' in England. The bishop of Bath received the gift of a horse from the archbishop of Armagh about 1434. A century before, in 1329, another English ecclesiastic, the prior of Christ Church, Canterbury, requested his agent to procure 'a good sure-footed mule' for him in Ireland. The transport of horses between Ireland and England was the subject of a law in 1471-2: no shipper was to charge more than 5s. for the freight of a horse, whereas before this, people had been charged up to one mark (13s. 4d.) for the journey. In 1507 the Irish parliament was ordered to pass a law prohibiting the export of any horses or *hobyes* to England, except by the king's subjects and through ports where there were customs officers. The sale of horses to Irish 'enemies' was always forbidden and, in this context, horses and arms were generally linked together.[20]

V

Ships and Mariners

TYPES OF TRADING AND FISHING VESSEL

The sea remains the same, and consequently change in ship design is always slow. Between 1200 and 1500 European ships continued to be made of wood and propelled by sails and oars, and the basic changes that did take place were aimed at increasing the capacity, speed and security of vessels. Difficulties begin immediately when one attempts to distinguish between different types of medieval ship. One English maritime historian notes forty-three varieties and stresses that the exact type of vessel described is often a matter of conjecture. For example, the word 'barge' is used in seven different ways in the fifteenth and early sixteenth century.

COG, which had come to mean 'a large ship' by the thirteenth century, is the term usually used to describe the typical sea-going

20 *Noah's Ark* (based on a sketch in the Book of Ballymote *c.* 1400, R.I.A. Dublin) This sturdy vessel with its heavy mast secured by shrouds, sternpost rudder and nailed planking represents a cog. Cogs would have been a common sight on the Atlantic coast of Ireland, shipping hides and fish throughout the Middle Ages.

vessel of northern Europe during the medieval period. It was single-masted with one large square sail. Sturdily built, its length to breadth proportion of about 3:1 made it a rather tubby vessel. Cogs varied in size — a collection of wine ships arrested at Southampton in 1326 included *La Cogge Johan* of 160 tons, with a crew of forty-seven, and *La Seintemaricogge* of sixty tons, which had a crew of twenty-two. The erratic nomenclature of medieval shipping occasionally includes the name and type of vessel and perhaps the name of the home port. If this information is accompanied by a detailed description of cargo and contents, then a reasonably accurate picture of the size of the vessel in question can be deduced. Thus most ships trading back and forth between Ireland and Bristol in the fourteenth and fifteenth centuries were not very big, since the average large cargo was approximately 20-30 tons and about half of that for the majority of small ships on the route.[1]

21 *Municipal seal of Youghal,* 1527 (*Council Book of the Corporation of Youghal,* 1878) This stylised representation shows the crescent shape of the hulk. The strong curved boards, fastened together by external pieces, were bound together at each end of the ship. Without stern or stern posts the vessel was steered by side rudders.

The HULK was originally crescent-shaped, without stem or stern posts but with ropes binding together the ends of the strong curved boards. It was driven by a large square sail and steered by side rudders, as depicted on the seals of many port towns. The *Blessed Mary* — a Waterford hulk — brought corn to the army in Gascony in 1297. In the later fifteenth century the term 'hulk' was applied to any large vessel, but especially to the large three masted ships of the Hanse that carried grain and timber from the Baltic, returning with salt from the Bay.

108

The BARGE was another type of ship which began to be distinguished around the beginning of the fifteenth century. Although details remain unclear, it appears that in England barges had a naval function serving as convoy escorts. They seem to have carried oars as well as sail and to have been about 50-100 tons in capacity. Barges sailed on commercial voyages also: *La barge Saint John* left Ireland with 8,400 hides in 1413 and in 1392 the king's council ordered the arrest of *bargeam de Vermewe de Spannya* in Ross and the re-arrest of a certain barge that broke arrest at Waterford and was then about to leave Drogheda with a cargo of merchandise for Irish enemies. A permit was given for Esmond Berle, a citizen of Dublin, in 1393 to purchase a barge from Gerald le Byrne, 'captain of his nation', as this was the only way he could recover his debts from the Irishman.[2]

The BALINGER was one of the commonest types of ship in use in the fifteenth century and may have originated in the Bay of Biscay, having evolved from an oared fishing boat to a two masted sailing vessel. It was between twenty and fifty tons in capacity and was used both for fishing and for the carriage of goods. It is most likely that balingers were 'the small cargo vessels from Brittany, the ubiquitous coasters of fifteenth-century northern Europe'. They were used for other purposes, too. A Breton 'balinger of war' captured a royal official in the Irish Sea in 1437 and took him off to be ransomed. In 1461 two Irish merchants were attacked and robbed near Winchelsea by pirates in a balinger. A balinger called the *Katerine* of Waterford, stated to have been of fifty tons burden, was arrested for the king's service in Bristol in 1414. In this connection balingers were used as transports, each carrying about forty soldiers. By this method of conscripting ships the English government solved its problem of transporting armies across the Channel or the Irish Sea. A fleet assembled in 1347 consisted of 738 ships manned by 15,000 sailors, which were required to transport 32,000 troops to the siege of Calais.[3]

Merchant ships increased in size in the latter part of the fifteenth century. The average displacement in the period 1461-83 was 159 tons. Carus-Wilson noted that this increase is shown in the Bordeaux customs accounts: the average cargo of Bristol ships using the port *c.* 1400 was eighty-eight tons, whereas it had risen to around 150 tons by 1450. By this time also the great CARRACKS appeared in northern waters. The carrack coming from an arabic word meaning 'cargo ship', represents the full development of the medieval ship. It had a full skeletal construction of ribs, which were covered with hull planking fitted edge to edge and not clinkered. There were two or three decks, with a large and high aftercastle and a smaller triangular forecastle. The ship had a rounded appearance and was broader at the waterline than at the deck. It carried three masts; the fore had one and the main-mast two square sails, and the mizzen-mast at the stern carried a lateen or triangular sail that enabled the ship to sail closer to the wind. It seems unlikely that many of these large ships would have had reason to call to Irish ports, although a Venetian carrack chartered by Italian and Aragonese merchants was captured on a voyage from Brittany to Dublin in 1431. In 1477 the ship of Bartholomew Couper of London, stated to have been of 320 tons, which took on board at New Ross 400 pilgrims bound for the shrine of St. James of Compostela, was most likely a carrack.

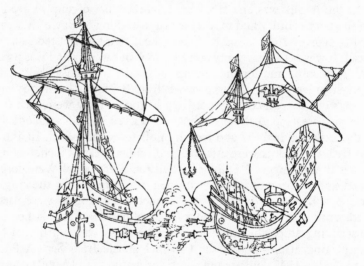

22 *Warships*, from John Goghe's map of Ireland, 1567 (*Cal. State Papers, Ireland 1509-1603*, Vol II) An exchange of fire between an English and a Scottish ship in the Irish Sea.

With some further, minor additions, such as the spritsail set under the bows, this vessel represents the full-rigged ship of the sixteenth century. A fine, lively drawing of two such vessels, equipped with guns, is depicted on John Goghe's map of Ireland (1567) and a woodcut of a naval battle in the 1577 edition of Holinshed's Irish chronicle is very similar in composition and shows the same type of ship fighting at close quarters.

The Goghe map also has a drawing of a CARAVEL shown sailing

off the southern Irish coast. The caravel was developed by the Portuguese and was long, low in the water and originally lateen-rigged throughout. Because of its rig it could sail very close to the wind and was useful for voyages up and down the west coast of Africa and to the Atlantic islands. A caravel with wine on board was at Passage East in Waterford harbour in 1438. In addition to their use as trading ships they were favoured by pirates because of their speed. A Breton caravel in association with a balinger captured a ship in the Irish Sea in 1456. During the sixteenth century the caravel reached its full development, carrying two square sails on its fore-mast and lateens on the main- and mizzen-masts.[6]

CRAYERS and PICKARDS were probably the most numerous sailing craft in Irish waters. They are first noted around the mid-fourteenth century and appear to be slightly smaller versions of the balinger. Both seem to have been connected with fishing. Several crayers were among the Bristol ships that came to Ireland *c.* 1400, bringing old wine, salt and cloth and returning with salmon. The *George* of Bristol

23 *Caravel*, from John Goghe's map of Ireland, 1567

was a crayer of less than twenty-eight tons. It carried four tons of old wine, twenty quarters of salt and eight seamen. The *Margaret* of Bristol was a crayer with a similar cargo, but was crewed by a master and twelve seamen. The *Trinity* of Bristol, which is also described as a crayer, carried twenty tons of old wine and a crew of sixteen. James Butler, earl of Ormond, occasionally hired a crayer called the *Gabriel* of Waterford when he had to go to England in the 1380s. For the longer journey to Gascony in 1338, Maurice, the

111

son of the earl of Desmond, hired a cog, *La Rodecogge*, of Limerick.[7]

Irish pickards are noted leaving Bridgewater and Minehead *c.* 1500 with small cargoes of salt or victuals and returning with fish. They appear to have been acting as 'lighters' for a fishing fleet. In 1403, when all the ships in the port of Ross were being arrested, pickards were excepted. A statute of 1465 for the licensing of boats fishing in Gaelic areas distinguishes between fishing boats of over twelve tons equipped with lighters and skiffs, and boats of less than twelve tons without lighters. These lighters may have been pickards, while the boats of over twelve tons were probably crayers. This appears to be verified by customs tolls at Ardglass in 1515, when boats 'with a top' were charged 5s. and every pickard or ship 'without a top' was charged 3s. 4d.[8]

Shipbuilding A considerable amount of shipbuilding took place in Irish ports during the later middle ages. There seems to be no reason to doubt that ships named as 'of' a particular port, for example the *Gabriel* of Waterford, were actually constructed in that port. Drogheda's murage grant of 1296 mentions tariffs on shipbuilding materials coming to the town: for every hundred large boards the charge was ¼d., for each mast ¼d., for every dozen ropes for rigging ¼d., for every hundred canvasses ½d.

Ireland did not lack the appropriate raw materials and 'shipboards' were exported. Nor does it seem likely that expertise was lacking: in the thirteenth century many mandates were issued by the king for galleys to be built in Irish ports. In 1234 six were ordered, two with sixty oars and four with forty oars and in 1241 the men of Drogheda were ordered to build a new galley to go with the one they had, Waterford was to build two, and Drogheda, Cork and Limerick one each. In 1298 William de Ware, a burgess of Cork, built a ship within the town and had to make a hole in the wall to get it to the river. Carpenters were employed in making modifications to wine ships in Dublin in 1332-3. In 1408 William Symcock and others were granted as many *cementarios* (builders) and other things necessary to help Janico Dartas to build a *nave de guerra* in Drogheda. There are references to ships being grounded for repairs in Waterford *c.* 1460, to a new mast being fitted to a ship in Kinsale in 1476-7, and municipal laws of Galway and Waterford forbade any boat-making materials to be sold to the Irish.[9]

In the fourteenth and fifteenth centuries ships were built by local craftsmen. Construction depended on 'secrets', in the form of measurements and models which were handed down through generations of skilled shipwrights. Apart from merchant ships and warships, hundreds of fishing boats, crayers and pickards must have been built, besides riverboats of all types, ferryboats, vessels used for transporting wood and other bulky materials, and fishing cots.[10]

In their use of ships in the course of normal trading activities, the merchants of the Irish ports were no different from their counterparts in England and in the non-Hanseatic ports of Europe. Sometimes they were shipowners and used their own vessels; sometimes they hired ships in their own home ports. At other times they chartered English or foreign ships when this was convenient.

In the early fourteenth century, on at least two occasions, a major requisitioning operation was launched in the Irish ports to assemble a fleet to carry an army to Scotland. In 1301 46 of the 74 vessels assembled were Irish and in 1303 about 37 of the 173 arrested were from the home ports. Towards the end of the fifteenth century some indication of the numbers of Irish ships emerges from the Bristol customs accounts. W. A. Childs has found that over the decade 1480-9 at least 70 and perhaps as many as 90 ships and at least 93 working shipmasters from Ireland called in at Bristol and Bridgewater. There were probably about 30 more operating on the Chester run, which shows that Ireland at that time was well provided with shipping on the two main trade routes to England.[11]

NAVIGATION AND SEA-CHARTS

The only navigational instrument of ancient times was the sounding lead. Apart from this the sailor followed landmarks and used his knowledge of the stars. The magnetized needle may have been used as a directional guide in Viking times, but its use when floating in a bowl of water became widespread in twelfth-century Europe. During the thirteenth century when the needle was fixed on a dry pivot and was combined with a card indicating the thirty-two points, it became a prototype of the mariner's compass. In the Mediterranean area sailors using this compass and an hour-glass were able to record sailing directions in detail. Notes of bearings and distances were complied and were called 'portulans'. 'Portulan maps' were an attempt to depict graphically these directions and appeared in Italy c. 1250. A medieval sea captain with such a book and map could, in theory, plot his course with some accuracy.

The early Italian portulans display a surprising knowledge of the Irish coast. One by Angelino Dulcert (1339) names over fifty places and islands in Ireland. Until about the mid-fifteenth century most portulans were copied from each other. No satisfactory explanation can be found as to how the compiler of the prototype came by his information, whether from Scandinavian or Irish sources, from the Italian merchant-banking companies or from wine traders.

Further study using the original maps led M.C. Andrews to distinguish several stages of development in the depiction of Ireland on the portulan charts. In the fifteenth century an important new type emerged that omitted a number of the names given on the earlier maps and added about thirty new ones. Among the latter were Malahide (*Malaida*) and Ardglass (*Argales*) on the east coast. Most of the new names were on the Atlantic coast, including Baltimore (*Beltario*), Galway (*Galuei*) and Sligo (*Slagoi*), which is an indication of the increase in commercial activity along the western coast due to the development of the herring fisheries and the growth of the wine trade with Spain and Portugal. Navigation using the charts alone, however, would have been hazardous since the depiction of the coastline was defective. The maps failed, for example, to show how Connacht jutted out into the Atlantic and perhaps this is one reason for the numerous Spanish Armada wrecks in this area in September 1588.[1]

The practical instructions given in late medieval books of sailing directions were very general and cannot have been of much use to anyone who had not already first-hand experience of the sea-area in question. One fifteenth-century English book of sailing directions, or 'rutter' as such books were called included instructions about the Irish coast. Mariners navigating between Spain and Ireland would have had access to the following information: 'Cape Fenister and Clere in Irlonde north and south' (i.e. south for the return voyage). Someone sailing to the Irish sea ports from England would have had the following information: 'Land's End and the toure of Waterford (the Hook Tower) north-north-west and south-south-west . . . for to clean of all the ground between Tuskar and Dalkey the course is north-

24 *Ireland*, from the Upsal map, *c*. 1450 (redrawn by T.J. Westropp,
R.I.A. Proc., xxxi, sect c, 1913)

east and south-south-west'. The notes continue in this fashion from
point to point around the coast. Some additional material is provided
about the tidal pattern off the south coast, but the information is
so sparse that it is little wonder that merchants rarely ventured into
unfamiliar waters without a pilot. In 1470 a balinger of Southampton
heading for Iceland was delayed in the Scilly Isles by bad weather,

115

until it was too late to sail north that year. The merchants decided
to go to Ireland instead and put into Mount's Bay in order to take
a new pilot experienced in Irish waters. Hanseatic merchants coming
from La Rochelle in 1387 were also afraid to come to Ireland without
a pilot.[2]

The information in the rutter probably served as a memory aid to
the pilot or master, reminding him, for instance, to beware of the
rock in the bay of Lough Swilly and on what side to leave the
Copeland Islands when approaching the Irish Sea from the north.
Pilots and shipmasters were sometimes negligent and risked the safety
of the ship and crew. John de Colecestre, a pilot (*lodmannus*), found
himself in prison in Dublin Castle in 1307 because 'he maliciously
and traitorously guided a ship upon Lambeye, so that it was
endangered with the victuals of the King'. A group of Irish merchants
complained that, while going from Dublin to Flanders, their ships
and the greater part of their merchandise were lost near Plymouth
'for lack of good ruling and by negligence of the masters'.[3]

Shipwreck and sea-travel Accounts of shipwrecks appear in the
records because of the law of wreck. By the statute of Westminster
(1295) it was agreed that if any man, dog or cat escaped alive out
of a ship, then neither the ship nor any of its goods could be adjudged
'wreck'. The sheriff was to hold the goods for a year and a day, in
order to see whether anyone could prove title to them. If not, they
went to the king. In 1335 a merchant of Cork was bringing wool
and other goods to Normandy in the *Rudecog* of Howth, when it was
driven ashore in Cornwall. He complained that certain Cornishmen
carried away merchandise, despite the fact that many mariners reached
land alive and that therefore the ship and cargo were not legally
'wreck'. Two Dublin merchants had difficulty reclaiming their goods
after their ship had been lost off Dungeness in 1401. The constable
of Dover had arrested some of the merchandise as wreck, although
the merchants and sailors were saved. In December 1559 the
Turtledove of Purmaren in Zeeland, en route from Spain to Antwerp,
was driven on to rocks near Fethard on the south coast of Wexford.
P.H. Hore quotes a long and detailed salvage agreement negotiated
between the shipowner, the shipper, locals who helped in the rescue,
and merchants from New Ross who eventually bought part of the
cargo.

Shipwrecks were frequent in the Irish Sea, an area which often

provided atrocious sailing conditions for medieval shipping. Giraldus
Cambrensis remarked that 'the Irish Sea, surging with currents that

25 *Michael Tregury,*
   Archbishop of Dublin,
   1449-71 (*Register of*
   wills, ed. Berry,
   frontispiece).

rush together, is nearly always tempestuous, so that even in summer
it scarcely shows itself calm even for a few days to them that sail'.
Getting from England to Ireland often meant weeks of waiting for
a suitable wind. *Laud's Annals* tell of John Curcie who in 1204
attempted fifteen times to sail over to Ireland 'but was always in danger
and the wind ever-more against him, wherefore he waited for a while
among the monks of Chester. At length, he returned into France and
there rested in the Lord'. In 1365 John de Troye, treasurer of Ireland,
while crossing from England lost 'horses, cloth, furs, coffers and all
else that he then had' in a storm. Michael Tregury, the archbishop-

117

elect of Dublin, lost his gold, silver, plate and jewels in the Irish Sea when crossing to take possession of his see *c.* 1450.[5]

Conditions were worst during the winter and, according to Hanseatic sea-laws, St. Martin's Day (11 November) was the end of the summer season for sailing. The case of a ship loaded with wines for Skinburness, which was blown around the north Irish sea in November and December 1306, has been noted earlier (above p. 00). Another ship with a similar cargo was wrecked at Portmarnock in December 1464. In December 1318 Edward II wrote to Pope John XXII excusing the failure of the new archbishops of Dublin and Cashel to attend the papal curia 'because the Irish Sea is so very perilous and stormy in winter'.[6]

Although there must have been considerably less traffic during the winter months, the Chester customs accounts show that smaller vessels from the Co. Dublin ports made frequent crossings in December and January. Familiarity with the area and the size of their boats meant that the sailors could take advantage of any break in the weather and bring their goods, which consisted mainly of fish, to Chester. Given favourable conditions the time necessary for the crossing was not great, and because of the prevailing westerly winds it was quicker from Ireland to England. Important news could travel quickly. Robin Frame notes that when Maurice FitzThomas, the first earl of Desmond died in Dublin on 25 January 1356, the English government ordered the taking of his lands into the king's custody in letters dated at Bamburgh, Northumberland, on 14 February. Bartholomew Rossynell, a Dublin merchant, told William of Worcester in 1479 that from the Isle of Man to Dublin was 'four *kennings** — a day and a night sailing'. Holyhead is stated to be three *kennings* or 60 miles from the Isle of Howth in Ireland. The distance between Dublin and Chester is practically the same as that between Dublin and the Isle of Man, but to follow the north Welsh coast made the Chester run a safer journey for smaller craft. William preserves a table of distances between Irish ports that Rossynell had given to him, besides a list of twenty havens in Ireland that he got from Thomas Howell de Lymerik.[7]

Some interesting travel details are given by Symon Semeonis, an Anglo-Irish Franciscan in his *Itinerarium*, which is an account of a pilgrimage that he made to the Holy Land in 1323. He and his companion, Hugh the Illuminator (*le Luminour*) left Clonmel, Co. Tipperary, on 16 March. They crossed 'the very stormy and

*a kenning was equal to about 21 nautical miles.

dangerous Irish Sea' and arrived at Chester on 24 April. After spending Easter at Chester where 'ships from Ireland arrive continuously', they journeyed overland through Coventry, 'most dear and useful to merchants', and on to London and Paris where they were amazed by the size of the cities. Crossing the Mediterranean they called at Crete and in an obvious reference to portulans Semeonis says: 'It is worthy of note that this island has a circuit of 500 miles according to the mariners who delineate the islands of the sea'. The account of their arrival at Alexandria has a contemporary ring about it. Their baggage was searched by Muslim officials, who were displeased with the religious images that Symon had in his possession. The friars had a long wait in Alexandria, until their papers were checked in Cairo and returned by carrier pigeon![8]

PIRACY OFF THE IRISH COASTS

The Scots on the Irish Sea   The Irish Sea area throughout the middle ages was a favourite hunting ground of pirates and sea rovers. St. Patrick's writings bear witness to their activities in the fifth century and raids by Irish pirates continued in the following centuries. The monks of Hartland, just beyond the north-eastern border of Cornwall, were given a manor in Devon where they might store their valuables 'in the summer time on account of the snares of Irish pirates'. The period of the Viking raids saw an increase in activity in the Irish Sea and dubious seafaring enterprises continued while the Norse dominated Man and the Isles. The kings of Scotland had suzerainty over the Isles in the years 1266-90 and 1313-33, but England, which held control in Man from 1290 to 1312, established permanent dominion over the island after 1333.[1]

Edward I and Edward II, in their campaigns against the Scots, depended on ships as their chief means of transport. Supplies and men were freighted north along the eastern and western coasts of England. Ireland's contribution was principally in the form of food supplies. These were shipped from the Irish ports, often in convoys, to Skinburness, the port of Carlisle, or to Ayr. English success in the first phase of the war, up to 1305, was due in part to Edward I's superior naval strength.

Between the death of Edward and the battle of Bannockburn the Scots increased their sea-power and 'Scottish enemies' operating in the north Irish Sea constantly preyed on the supply ships, despite the government's strenuous efforts to protect the vital provisions. Thomas Dun was Bruce's naval champion. He effectively controlled the Irish Sea north of Holyhead until he was captured and killed by John de Athy, the King's admiral, in 1317. Carrickfergus, a walled town with a strong castle on the shore of Belfast Lough, was frequently the government's base of naval operations. In 1319 five ships that had been provided by the county of Devon were to be delivered to John de Athy, constable of Carrickfergus, 'for repelling the Scots'. When John was replaced as admiral by Roger de Leyburn in 1322, he was ordered to deliver all the ships in his custody to his successor, except those that he needed for the custody of Carrickfergus. Later that year the justiciar was ordered to keep supplies safely near the coast until de Leyburn came to convey them to Scotland 'as the sea between the land of Man, Ireland and Skinburness is infested by the King's enemies with the intention of taking the victuals'.[2]

In 1310-2 and in 1315-6 payments were made to shipmasters whose vessels were on duty in the north Irish Sea. The constable of a Drogheda ship was paid 12d. a day and thirty mariners 3d. each day for twenty-four days' naval service in 1310-2. In 1315-6 the master and constable of the *Aliceot* of Bristol received £30 in wages for half a year's service 'to overcome the Scots and Irish . . . our felons and enemies by the sea coasts'.[3]

The failure of the English to control the high seas and to enforce a blockade was one reason for their lack of success in Scotland. All through the later middle ages Scottish warships continued to menace merchants and other shipping, particularly on the northern Irish Sea. Robert de Stokis, a merchant of Drogheda, was captured in the area in 1337 and brought to Dumbarton Castle. His ransom was to be in the form of victuals worth forty marks. In 1345-7 John of Lyons, returning from trading in Connacht, was driven by storm to the Scottish coast. There his ship was captured by rebels. What followed was typical and may offer one reason for the constant attacks of the Scots. When hostages were taken, John and his ship were sent to Drogheda to bring back food supplies by way of ransom. The Scots of the Isles and the west coast were in constant need of victuals and raided frequently in search of them. When English ships were captured, similar ransom demands were made.

The community of the Isle of Man must have suffered much through loss of trade because of the Scots. In 1342, however, with the consent of the earl of Salisbury, Manxmen arranged a year's truce with the Scots to allow merchants of England, Ireland and Wales to come safely to the island. The fine paid to the Scots for this truce included, besides money, wheat, horses and cows.[4] In 1385-6 a force of ships was assembled in Drogheda 'on account of the depredations of the Scottish enemies on the coast'.

Expeditions like this one, and the building of the galley in Drogheda in 1408-9, were probably motivated mainly by fear of the political alliances between the Irish chieftains of Ulster and the Scots of the Isles. In 1433, for example, Eoghan Ó Néill in his war with O'Donnell and the Anglo-Irish of Meath had the support of a Scottish fleet, which burnt the town of Ardglass Co. Down and sailed around the north-east coast to the Inishowen peninsula to link up with the main O'Neill army and exact submission from O'Donnell.[5]

The merchants of the east coast and of Drogheda in particular looked to their own welfare and, undeterred by political conflict, appear to have had important business relations with the Gaelic Irish of Ulster and with the Scots. Around 1400, Drogheda merchants had control of the valuable Bann fishery and also sailed to Ulster to buy cattle for the meat store of the town. Later in the fifteenth century they arranged safe conducts for themselves through the archbishop of Armagh (whose main residence at this time was near Drogheda). In 1443 a safe-conduct for a Drogheda merchant was negotiated with Donal Ballagh, Lord of the Isles. In 1463 safe-conducts for a group of merchants were obtained from Henry O'Neill — for safe access to the ports in his *comitatus et patria*.

Many of the hazards that medieval merchants and mariners faced on the Irish Sea are illustrated by the following account preserved in the register of Archbishop Octavian of Armagh. It is based on the testimony of James Ylane, an educated man (*litteratus*), given in Drogheda on 2 September 1473. Robert Clement, a townsman of Drogheda, was taking his ship to Pembroke in Wales. On board were James Ylane, Thomas Rede with his wife and sons, Cornelius O'Duhy and his companions who had merchandise for sale, and others. Having embarked on the ship, they crossed over to Holyhead and anchored there to wait for a suitable wind. Some local Welshmen came out to the ship and the Redes went ashore with them. O'Duhy and his friends asked Robert to run them ashore in the ship's boat but he refused because, he explained, there was a quarrel at that time between the men of Dublin and Drogheda and the locals of Anglesea, and he would not risk losing his boat, which was worth 40s. It was said on board that in fact the Redes were robbed as soon as they set foot in Wales. The following night, Robert sent two of his crewmen ashore in the boat with flour to make bread, but early next morning, before they had returned, a favourable wind arose and Robert sailed away from Holyhead, leaving the boat and the two men behind. Later the weather worsened and ship, caught in a bad storm was tossed hither and thither. O'Duhy and his companions were so alarmed that when they reached St. Davids they asked to be put ashore, preferring, as they put it, to lose their goods rather than their lives. The shipmaster put them ashore there, along with some Welshmen who were aboard, telling them that they would be safe going ashore at St. Davids since it was a place of pilgrimage and they could claim to be pilgrims.

O'Duhy and his company decided to continue overland to Pembroke from there as they had had enough of the sea and when they did arrive in the town they began to sell their wares —'faldings', or mantles, and knives (*cultellos*). James Ylane was staying at an inn in Pembroke when a messenger came for him saying that the steward of the castle wanted to see him, to ask of news (*novos rumores*) from Ireland. James was suspicious but when he saw others from the castle, along with the Welshmen who had sailed with them, rounding up O'Duhy and his companions he became frightened and fled into a church for sanctuary. Later he got away and travelled to Oxford. The others, it appears, were kept under guard in the castle for nine or ten weeks. James Ylane testified that he did not know what part, if any, the shipowner Robert Clement played in all of this, except that he knew for certain that Robert was still in Pembroke three days after the others had been imprisoned in the castle.[6]

Bretons and Spaniards on the Irish Sea   Increasing numbers of Breton and Spanish pirates began to appear after 1400 in the southern Irish Sea. In 1437 the cathedral town of St. Davids in Wales was so menaced by pirates that the citizens resolved to attack them and got help from the clerics of the cathedral. In 1442 Drogheda petitioned for money to repair its walls, complaining that Spanish, Scottish and other rebels daily frequented the coasts of Ireland, destroying ships and merchants. The men of Waterford complained in the same year of attacks by enemies, including Scots, Bretons and Spaniards, and instanced the

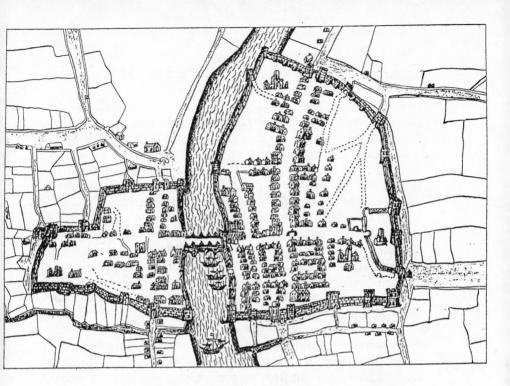

26 *Drogheda*, 1657 (The Irish Architectural Archive, Dublin) This
mid-seventeenth-century plan by Robert Newcomen gives a good
impression of the medieval town of Drogheda. There were in fact
two towns, separated by the river Boyne, one in Co. Meath and
the other in Co. Louth until they were united in 1412 (facsimile
by Mr Nicholas Sheaff).

loss of a ship of Flanders that was taken by Bretons with goods worth
4,000 marks. Walter Dolman, carrying letters from the king to the
lieutenant and chancellor of Ireland, was captured by Bretons in the
Irish Sea in August 1437. He spent twelve months in prison in
Brittany and paid a £200 ransom.

The Scots demanded victuals by way of ransom, but the Bretons
were more interested in money and had evolved a system by which
ransoms were paid that had a quasi-legal standing. An incident in
1446 illustrates the procedures involved. A group that included two
proctors of Llanthony Priory was captured at sea by two Breton ships.
The prisoners were divided between the ships and ransoms were
agreed upon. Certain men became in effect hostages and were taken
off to Brittany to be held until those who were freed raised all of
the ransom money. One of these men, Davy Fleming, had to sue
through Parliament some of his companions who had been freed,

since they did not pay the Bretons fully and he had to make up a substantial deficit in order to go free.[7]

The fifteenth century saw also an increase in normal trading contact between Ireland and Brittany, and Breton merchant ships frequented the Irish Sea. Often these paid for the depredations of their fellow countrymen. Arising from a petition of a Hanseatic merchant who had been robbed, there was a general licence to arrest Breton ships in Irish ports in 1412. In 1421 Drogheda merchants sought and obtained safe-conducts for Breton merchants and their ships to come with goods to Ireland. It would appear, however, that Breton shipping was considered by some seafarers to be 'fair game'.

Again the registers of the archbishops of Armagh provide a clear illustration, for on 1 July 1484 Primate Octavian himself witnessed a seemingly unprovoked attack on Breton shipping in Drogheda harbour. Having been told by members of his household that three ships were coming into port he climbed up the tower of his manor in Termonfechin, which is about a mile from the sea, and saw the vessels mooring in the harbour. Over a period of about four hours, he observed them lying 'peacefully and quietly' with sails furled and anchors planted. Then from the south came two ships of Liverpool 'running under sail with great haste'. These ships he recognised as belonging to John Byrron, lieutenant of the Lord of the Isle of Man. The Breton ships were undefended, since their crews had gone into Drogheda for recreation and some of the archbishop's friends had seen them in town. John Byrron's sailors seized two of the Breton vessels, the *Mighell* of Garrant and the *Katheryne* of Croswyk, which were laden with iron, salt and wine, and took them away with all their merchandise.[8]

Government measures against piracy were fairly thorough in the early fourteenth century, when the king's power was strong on both sides of the sea and when important military supplies were required. Later there were some sporadic attempts at concerted naval activity. An expedition of over fifty ships carrying a large force including both the earl of Ormond and the earl of Desmond, sailed from Drogheda to the Isles in 1335 under the command of Janico Dartas. Ships were arrested to go against the Scots in 1385-6 and admirals were appointed in 1414. The government may have been forced into renewed activity against pirates in the mid-fifteenth century as a result of a shocking event. This was the abduction of Michael Tregury, the archbishop of Dublin. In 1454 he was captured in Dublin Bay by pirates and taken to Ardglass in Co. Down, from where a hastily mobilized fleet rescued him. A plan to provide ships to guard the area north of

Wicklow Head was launched in 1454-5. The expense of these ships was to be met by a levy on merchant ships and fishing boats, which was to be collected in the ports of the area. This levy was renewed in 1460 for a further three years.[9]

In 1467-8 there were plans to fortify Lambay Island, a few miles north of Dublin Bay because 'Bretons, French, Spaniards and Scots were harboured there. This seemingly had not been done by 1496-7

27 *A naval battle* (Holinshead's *Irish Chronicle*, 1577) 'At Whisuntide in the yeare 1400 whiche was the first yeare of the raigne of Henry the fourth, the Conestable of Dublin Castell, and diuerse other, at Stranford in Vlster fought by Sea with Scottes, where many English men were slaine and drowned.'

when another plan was presented. This time the abbot of Holmpatrick proposed to build a fortified harbour, a work of stone and wood, between Skerries and the Isle of Mellock. He was granted the income from the various customs and poundages of Skerries to help him.

The disorder and piracy in the Irish Sea continued in the sixteenth century. In 1515-17 Henry VIII established an admiralty office at Beaumaris, in an attempt to deal with a problem that was to persist fifty years later. A drawing illustrating the map of John Goghe (1567) shows an English and a Scottish ship blasting away at each other at close range in the Irish Sea. The Scots can be seen preparing a huge grappling hook while men in both ships armed with swords and spears prepare to board.[10]

125

Piracy off the Southern and Western coasts The political state of south Munster and the west of Ireland in the later middle ages was disorderly. If the influence of the central administration in the Irish Sea area was weak, it was practically non-existent along the sea coast west of Waterford. Important sea routes near the south and west of Ireland were frequented by a variety of merchants and their vessels: wine ships coming from Gascony and Spain, England and Irish merchants trading in hides, fishing vessels from the west of England, and merchant venturers on the Iceland route all sailed within sight of the southern and western coasts of Ireland.

Intermittent warfare between Spain and England meant frequent attacks on merchant shipping, particularly in the southern coastal area in the fourteenth century. In 1356 some Cork merchants had freighted the *Seinte Marie* of Castro Urdiales (in Castile) to bring goods belonging to them from Bordeaux to Cork. The owner and his crew deliberately put into a harbour in Brittany, where the cargo was seized and the merchants' agents held to ransom. Waterford had received a grant in 1377 to repair and enclose its quays because of the danger of attacks by various enemies, including Spaniards. The same year a Bristol ship sheltering from a storm in Kinsale was arrested because four or five of the seamen on board were Spanish.

In 1380 the Spaniards posed a very real threat to the southern ports when part of a fleet of French and Spanish galleys whose crews had been raiding the English coast, appeared at Kinsale. They were set upon in the harbour by sailors from a number of English and Irish ships. In the battle that followed, 400 of the foreigners were reputed to have been killed, fourteen of their captains and five of their ships captured, and twenty-one English vessels recovered. A year later Kinsale applied for, and was granted, the income from certain customs to fortify the town.[11]

Admirals were appointed for the ports of Co. Cork in 1381-2. Inspired perhaps by the recent victory over the foreign galleys, they attempted to deal with another menace to merchant shipping in the area. The admirals were commissioned 'to fight with God's assistance the nation of the O'Driscolls, Irish enemies, who constantly remained upon the western ocean' preying on passing ships. How the admirals fared is obscure, but the well-known feud between the city of Waterford and the O'Driscolls had begun by this time. The raids and counter-raids of this quarrel became part of the folklore of sixteenth-century Munster and were noted in detail by the compiler of the Book of Howth.

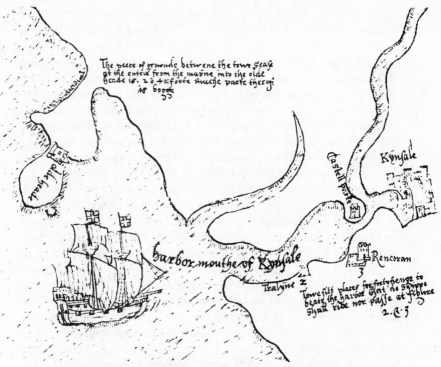

The writing within the map reads:

The peece of grownde betwene the town geate of the entrie from the marine into the olde hedde is. 2.0 4 o:foote muche parte therof is boggie

harbor mouthe of Kynsale

Kynsale

Castell perse

Rencoran

Tralyne 2

Lowe fift places for fortyfienge to beate the harbor that no shippe shall ride nor passe at fibie 2.Q.3

28   *Kinsale Harbour*, 1587 (N.L.I. Ms 2656 in *Ulster & Other Irish Maps*, ed. G.A. Hayes-McCoy)   This detail is taken from a map of Cork and Kinsale harbours which has written on the back 'The plotte of the Olde hedd of Kingsall the haven of Kingsall and the haven of Corke wt other necessary places to be fortefied.'

The O'Malleys of Connacht, whose lordship included Achill and many islands in Clew Bay, occasionally indulged in sea roving. While returning from a successful expedition in 1396 with a ship full of valuables Conchobhar, the son of Eóghan Ó Máille, was drowned between Ireland and Aran. A branch of the O'Briens, who controlled the Aran Islands, maintained a fleet which, according to Hardiman, kept Galway free of pirates in return for an annual tribute of wine. There is some reason to suspect the integrity of these protectors, for in 1400 Nicholas Kent of Galway was licensed to recruit a naval force in Bristol to free the city from William de Burgo and to take the Aran Islands, 'which always lie full of galleys for the spoiling of the king's lieges'. Some years later, an English ship leaving Galway was attacked and robbed. Sailors on the same ship had repelled an attack by certain Irish earlier on this voyage.[12]

The citizens of Limerick looked to their own protection by building in 1505 'a great tri-oared galley fitted out with all things necessary'. Galleys at this time carried three oarsmen to a bench, usually under 40 metres long with a width one-eighth of their length. They had about 24 benches to each side and were fitted with a single mast carrying a lateen sail. By 1500 this Mediterranean-type of warship was in use all over Europe, even as far north as Finland and its principal weapon then consisted of a single heavy bronze cannon set along the centre line at the bow. Such a highly manoeuverable, oared galley would be a particularly suitable vessel for patrolling the sixty miles of estuary between the city of Limerick and the sea. The Shannon estuary was of doubtful value as a haven for medieval ships. In fact the only safe anchorage between Valentia Island and Galway was the port of Dingle, which was under the jurisdiction of the earl of Desmond. Ships taking refuge there from Atlantic gales sometimes faced other dangers. The *Trinity* of Bristol, which was heading for Limerick in 1401 with wine, salt and honey, was robbed of goods valued at 1,000 marks while sheltering in Dingle. The owner could get no redress from the earl of Desmond, perhaps because the White Knight, the sheriff of Desmond and other notables were involved.

Nicholas Arthur (*c.* 1405-65) a prominent merchant of Limerick fared better regarding compensation. He had left Limerick for England with various goods worth 700 marks freighted on a ship of John Church of London in the summer of 1428. *En route* Bretons captured the vessel, took it to St. Malo and there auctioned off the ship and cargo. Nicholas they kept imprisoned in Mont St.-Michel for two years until he paid a ransom of 400 marks. On his release he got letters of reprisal against any Bretons 'within the dominions of the king of England whether by land or by sea' to the value of 8,000 marks, which reprisals, we are told, 'he bravely, energetically and perseveringly levied even to the last farthing and wrested from them perforce'.[13]

Kinsale in the fifteenth century grew to be a prosperous port, but 'freebooting made it notorious rather than famous'. The mayor of Bristol was ordered to arrest all ships and merchants of Kinsale in 1447, because an English ship had been captured by one John Galway from that town. A Bristol fishing boat that had captured a Spanish merchant ship in 1449 was itself attacked by a fleet of vessels from Kinsale and taken back to that port. There it was disposed of, along with its prize. Freebooters seemed to have found in Kinsale a haven and a ready market for stolen goods. In 1477, a merchant ship sailing towards Youghal was attacked off Bantry Bay by an English boat

128

from Minehead in Somerset. The attackers despoiled the captive ship and made for Kinsale, where they put the crew ashore naked and presumably disposed of the booty in the town. Sir Richard Edgecombe arrived in the port in 1488 searching for one Con Eop, 'a rover upon the sea'. Kinsale's reputation lived on into the next century, when it was used by Francis Drake and others in the golden age of English buccaneering.[14]

Conclusion

About the year 1300, Ireland was a prosperous country with an economy based chiefly on agricultural production. Merchants of the principal ports bought, sold and exchanged goods in a hinterland that was to a large extent populated by tenants of manorial farms, many of whom had come from England and Wales. Two hundred years later, Ireland also had a healthy economy, but on a quite different basis. By this time a considerable trade had developed in products associated with fish, cattle and sheep and the local clientele of the merchants now comprised mostly Irish and Anglo-Irish lords and their followers. By 1500 the economy had adapted itself to the almost continuous warfare and political unrest that characterised later medieval Ireland.

The general pattern of trade between 1300 and 1500 shows that the imports and exports of medieval Ireland were, with one important exception, managed by wealthy merchant families in the ports, who enjoyed an importance out of all proportion to their numbers. It is also clear that the prosperity of the merchants and the towns was completely dependent on relations with the local Irish and Anglo-Irish. Hides, wool, fish, flax and furs all came from outside the town walls; so also did essential supplies of corn, meat, fuel and building materials. The townspeople in their turn offered wine, salt, iron and fine cloth to the population of the hinterland and a market for their produce in England and on the continent. The net result was an interdependence of producers and merchants that transcended politics, demonstrating that although politically there were two nations in later medieval Ireland, economically there was only one.

The merchants by and large were undeterred by local political strife and sometimes capitalised on it. With a weak central administration they were able to exploit their position as loyal citizens to secure privileges that made the ports, especially in the south and west, virtual city-states. Frequently these merchants ignored prohibitions on trading with enemies and rebels at home, while they always protested their loyalty and status as royal subjects in commercial dealings abroad.

130

The constant cries of distress and economic ruin which were voiced by the citizens of the Irish ports in the later middle ages are belied as much by descriptions of the wealth and prosperity of the same towns left by sixteenth-century visitors, as by entries in English port books and the findings of customs officials.

It appears that all the Irish ports did not follow the same trading pattern throughout the fourteenth and fifteenth centuries and that in particular the ports of the Pale area were a separate entity. There was little basic change in the economy of Dublin and Drogheda between 1300 and 1500, mainly because there was no major change in the economic pattern of the hinterland. Counties Meath, Dublin and Louth, although diminished in size and enclosed by the Pale, remained centres of agricultural production much as they had been. The men of Dublin and of Drogheda, individually and through their newly constituted guilds, were among the most enterprising of medieval Irish merchants. Despite the great drawbacks caused by silting, which also affected their counterparts in Chester, the merchants of both towns kept abreast of developments in fifteenth-century trading patterns. They shipped corn to the southern towns, freighted large ships from Brittany and Spain, sailed to Ulster and Scotland with victuals and even ventured to Iceland.

The greatest single economic event of the two centuries was the arrival of the herring shoals off the south-western and western coasts. The prosperity brought by the herring benefited chiefly the Irish and Anglo-Irish lords whose lands bordered the fishing grounds, and indirectly the merchants of the towns. There was a new phase of building tower-houses and fine halls in western Ireland and the wealth that the herring brought to the area offers an explanation for the endowments of many new houses for Observantine friars. Later in the sixteenth century, when the fishing was concentrated off the Donegal coast, the money accruing from landing rights and other dues enabled O'Donnell and his neighbours to equip and train substantial armies.

The trade and relative prosperity shared by the citizens of the towns and the magnates of the countryside in Ireland *c.* 1500 continued and increased for a time in the sixteenth century, but it was not to last. During the reign of Henry VIII and particularly in Elizabethan times, systematic and ruthless warfare, accompanied by the displacement of people, wasted the countryside on which the prosperity of all depended. A strong central government eventually crushed the independence of both lords and merchants and effectively brought the middle ages in Ireland to an end.

131

Notes and References

CHAPTER I

Corngrowing and the grain trade

1 Cf. Frank Mitchell, *The Shell Guide to Reading the Irish Landscape* (Dublin, 1986), pp 173-9; A. J. Otway-Ruthven, 'The Organisation of Anglo-Irish agriculture in the Middle Ages' in *R.S.A.I. Jn.*, lxxxi (1951), p. 1. Most recently a close examination of the nature of the Anglo-Norman settlement has been made showing how both greater and lesser lords carefully planned and organised agriculture on their estates cf. C. A. Empey 'Conquest and settlement; patterns of Anglo-Norman settlement in north Munster and south Leinster' in *Ir. Econ. & Soc. Hist.*, xiii (1986), pp 5-37; Kevin Down, 'Colonial society and economy' in *N.H.I.*, II, p. 471.

2 *Cal. doc. Ire.*, *1293-1301*, nos. 570, 716, 836; J. F. Lydon *Ireland in the later Middle Ages* (Dublin, 1973), pp 9-10; Bolton, *English Economy*, pp 32-4, 242ff; cf. Fernand Braudel, *The structures of everyday life*, Vol I of *Civilization and capitalism, 15th-18th century* (London 1981; 1985), pp 120ff; Richard W. Unger, *The Ship in the Medieval Economy, 600-1600* (London & Montreal, 1980), p. 163.

3 *Stat. Ire. John to Hen. V*, p. 517; R.I.A. 24/H/17, p. 47; C. A. Empey, 'The Butler Lordship' in *Jn. of the Butler Society*, iii (1970-1), pp 184-5; Hore, *Wexford Town*, V. p. 120; *Rot. pat. Hib.*, p. 136 nos 197, 201, 202.

4 See J. J. Bagley, *Historical Interpretation: Sources of English Medieval History 1066-1540* (Middlesex, 1965), pp 122-4; *Cal. doc. Ire.*, *1302-7*, pp 42, 75, 125, *Cal. pat. rolls 1307-13*, pp 13, 194, 509, *ibid.*, *1317-21* p. 38, *ibid.*, *1321-4* p. 288; *Cal. close rolls*, *1381-5*, p. 158.

5 e.g. *Cal. pat. rolls*, *1313-17*, p. 219; *ibid.*, *1321-4*, p. 298, *ibid.*, *1340-3*, p. 124, *ibid.*, *1343-5*, p. 3; *ibid.*, *1354-8*, p. 286, *Rot. pat. Hib.*, (1374) p. 89, no. 121, *ibid.*, (1401) p. 164, no. 155; Aubrey Gwynn & R. N. Hadcock *Medieval Religious Houses: Ireland*, (London, 1970), p. 128; Eric St. John Brooks 'Fourteenth century monastic estates in Meath: the Llanthony cells of Duleek and Colp' in *R.S.A.I. Jn.*, lxxxiii (1953) *passim*; *Cal. pat. rolls*, *1350-4*, p. 415, *ibid.*, *1377-81*, p. 61.

6 *Cal. pat. rolls.*, *1313-17*, p. 218; *ibid.*, *1321-4*, p. 39; Down *op. cit.* p. 479; *Cal. pat. rolls*, *1350-4*, p. 242; *ibid.*, *1374-7*, p. 251; *Rot. pat. Hib.*, p. 62, no. 110; N.S.B. Gras *The Evolution of the English Corn Market from the twelfth to the eighteenth century*, (Cambridge, 1915), p. 135.

7 Lydon, 'Ireland's participation', pp 192-7, 226-9; *Cal. doc. Ire.*, *1293-1301*, p. 270, no. 565; Calculation based on yields of the manor of Cloncurry in 1304, after figures by Kevin Down, allowing for seed corn and assuming the quarter equalled the Irish crannock and that the medieval acre was more than double the statute acre; *P.R.I. rep. D.K. 42*, p. 65.

8 Lydon, *Lordship,* pp 136-7. Detailed account of incidents in P.R.O.I. IA/53/29, ff 622, 625, 631; *Cal. pat. rolls, 1321-4,* p. 94; There were occasional requisitions e.g. *Cal. close rolls, 1349-54,* p. 456, *ibid., 1354-60,* p. 5.

9 *P.R.I. Rep. D.K. 38,* pp 29ff. and 44ff.; *Cal. close rolls, 1343-6,* p. 284; *Cal. justic. rolls Ire., 1305-7,* p. 158, cf. P.R.O.I. IA/53/28, p. 425 and Braudel, *op. cit.* pp 126-7; *Cal. pat. rolls, 1348-50,* p. 34.

10 See E.A. Lewis *Medieval Boroughs of Snowdonia* (London, 1912), pp 209ff; *Cal. pat. rolls, 1313-17,* p. 439; R.I.A. 12/D/13, p. 123; *Cal. pat. rolls, 1330-4,* p. 180; *Rot. pat. Hib.,* p. 96, nos. 220-2; *Cal. pat. rolls, 1374-7,* p. 393; *Rot. pat. Hib.,* p. 220, no. 85; Lewis, *op. cit.* p. 211.

11 *Cal. pat. rolls, 1307-13,* pp 10, 45; *ibid., 1321-4,* p. 204; *Cal. close rolls, 1343-6,* p. 16; *ibid., 1354-60,* p. 178; cf. *Rot. pat. Hib.,* p. 162, no. 102.

12 Exchequer Rolls of Scotland, i, pp 69, 186; *Cal. Carew MSS, Book of Howth,* p. 385; Michael Dolley, *Medieval Anglo-Irish Coins* (London, 1972), p. 62; *Rot. pat. Hib.,* p. 95, nos. 192-4, *ibid.,* p. 201, no. 121, no. 111.

13 Cf. John Dalton and J. R. O'Flanagan *History of Dundalk and its environs* (Dublin, 1864), p. 70; R.I.A. 12/D/12, p. 145; *Rot. pat. Hib.,* p. 97 no. 230, *ibid.,* p. 95, no. 201; *Cal. pat. rolls, 1374-7,* p. 303; *Rot. pat. Hib.,* p. 115, no. 225; *ibid.,* p. 161, no. 53 and p. 193, no. 172. Northburgh, on the Foyle, was another outpost which had to be maintained — cf. Robin Frame *English Lordship in Ireland, 1318-1361* (Oxford, 1982), p. 146.

14 *Cal. close rolls, 1374-7,* p. 11; *Rot. pat. Hib.,* p. 162, no. 106; *ibid.,* p. 193, no. 166; *ibid.,* p. 170, no. 74.

15 Braudel, *op. cit.,* p. 143; Hore, *Wexford town,* V, p. 120; *Rot. pat. Hib.,* p. 97, no. 229; *ibid.,* p. 96, nos. 223-5 — William of Windsor and his force were in the Munster area in 1375 and this must have increased the demand for supplies.

16 *Rot. pat. Hib.,* p. 136, nos. 185, 196, 188, 197, 201, 202; *ibid.,* p. 146, no. 217 — An interesting account of detailed regulations for the sale of corn in Cork in 1334 is given in an article by 'Sean Ghall' — 'Food control in medieval Ireland' in *Irish Theological Quarterly* XIII (1918), pp 106ff — unfortunately the primary sources are not cited; *Proc. king's council, Ire., 1392-3,* p. 120; *Rot. pat. Hib.,* (1408-9), p. 194, no. 189, (1422), p. 220, no. 100, cf. *Council Book of Kinsale* ed. Richard Caulfield, (Guilford, 1897), p. XII; *Stat. Ire. Hen. VI,* pp 171; 239, see also *Stat. Ire. 1-12 Edw IV* p. 139.

17 *Cal. pat. rolls, 1364-7,* p. 72; *Rot. pat. Hib.,* 179, no. 25; *ibid.,* p. 220, nos. 95, 106; *Cal. close rolls, 1374-7,* p. 491.

18 *Cal. pat. rolls, 1350-4,* p. 253; *ibid.,* p. 346; *ibid.,* p. 320. In these instances the exporters were ordered to bring back letters of discharge to the Irish chancery showing where the grain was unloaded.

19 *Gesta Pontificum* (Rolls ser.) p. 308 cited in Gras, *op. cit.,* p. 100 n; *Cal. pat. rolls, 1321-4,* p. 27 and cf. *Chester Customs* pp 110-13; Gras, *ibid.,* p. 101, also M. M. Postan 'The economic and political relations of England and the Hanse from 1400 to 1475' in *Studies in English Trade in the Fifteenth century* ed. E. Power and M. M. Postan (London, 1933), p. 140.

20 *Proc. King's council, Ire., 1392-3,* p. 175; *Rot. pat. Hib.,* (1404), p. 178, no. 67; *ibid.,* (1432), p. 256, no. 137; *ibid.,* (1451), p. 266, no. 24; *ibid.,* (1405), p. 181, no. 32 and (1412), p. 201, no. 116; *ibid.,* (1412), p. 201, no. 112 and (1414), p. 202, no. 17.

21 1456, *Stat. Ire. Hen. VI*, p. 447; 1410; *Stat. Ire. John-Hen V*, p. 527, 1462, *Stat. Ire. 1-12 Edw IV*, p. 5; *Stat. Ire. John-Hen V*, p. 293, *Rot. pat. Hib.*, p. 57, nos. 130, 144.

22 *Cal. close rolls, 1360-4*, p. 255; *ibid., 1364-8*, p. 453 and cf. A. J. Otway-Ruthven *History of Medieval Ireland* (London, 1968), p. 296; *Cal. close rolls, 1392-6*, p. 219, Hore, *Wexford town* I p. 215; *Rot. pat. Hib.*, p. 234, nos. 26, 42; *Cal. pat. rolls, 1396-9*, p. 119.

23 The sheriff of Meath was himself in court in 1315-6 for allowing a ship with corn to go to Scotland from his baliwick — R.I.A. 12/D/8, p. 411; P.R.O.I. IA/53/30, pp 31, 107, 124, 144; cf. R.I.A. 12/D/12, p. 154; *Stat. Ire. 1-12 Edw IV*, p. 853.

24 Giraldus Cambrensis *Expugnatio Hibernica* ed. A. B. Scott & F. X. Martin (Dublin, 1978), p. 35; see above p. 21. *Annals of Ireland by Friar John Clyn* ed. Richard Butler (Dublin, 1849), p. 22.

25 *Cal. pat. rolls, 1330-4*, p. 80; R.I.A. 12/D/14, p. 49; *Cal. close rolls, 1330-3*, p. 275; *Cal. pat. rolls, 1330-4*, p. 232; *ibid.*, pp 20, 429, 430, 487; *ibid.*, p. 75, 431. *Cal. close rolls, 1330-3*, p. 140. See also P.R.O. S.C. 8/32/1596.

26 Many of the debts owed to the Arthurs, merchants of Limerick *c.* 1380 were calculated in corn — Arthur MS p. 4ff. *Stat. Ire. Hen VI*, pp 236-7; Childs & O'Neill 'Overseas Trade' p. 503.

The fish trade

1 Cf. C. H. Younge, 'Fisheries in History: The Tunny, the Herring and the Cod; in *History Today*, xxv (1975), pp 334 ff; *Stat. Ire., 1-12 Edw IV*, p. 665.

2 Bolton, *English Economy* p. 276; A. R. Bridbury, *England and the Salt Trade in the Middle Ages* (Oxford, 1955), p. xvi.

3 *Cal. Justic. rolls Ire., 1305-7*, p. 279; T. E. McNeill *Anglo-Norman Ulster* (Edinburgh, 1980). He suggests that 'Tevere' is Tara in the Ards peninsula. p. 41; *Cartularies of St Mary's Abbey, Dublin*, ed. J. T. Gilbert, 2 vols. (Rolls Ser. 1884-6) I, p. 307; *Stat. Ire., 12-33 Edw. IV*, p. 389; *Chester Customs, passim*, See account for 1404-5, pp 103-116. Merchants of Chester and North Wales complained of harassment by Irish ministers in the early fourteenth century. P.R.O. S.C. 8/38/1888.

4 *Rot. pat. Hib.*, p. 136, no. 198; *ibid.*, p. 174, no. 71.

5 *Stat. Ire., John-Hen. V*, p. 399, see also regulations of 1430 in *Cal. close rolls, 1429-35*, p. 69; P.R.O.I. 1A/53/30, p. 90.

6 Hore, *Wexford town*, I, p. 213; *Proc. King's Council, Ire., 1392-3*, p. 163; Lydon, *Ireland in the Later Middle Ages*, p. 113. Sometimes it seems that English merchants accompanied a newly appointed lieutenant to Ireland to help with victualling. In 1430 a shipman, a spicer, skinner and butcher were given letters of protection — *Cal. pat. rolls, 1429-36*, pp 108, 109, 111, 330, 328 and 338.

7 D. B. Quinn 'Anglo Irish Ulster in the early sixteenth century' in *Belfast Nat. Hist. Proc.*, (1933-4), pp 61-3; Longfield *Anglo-Irish Trade*, p. 42; *Cal. Carew. MSS, 1515-74*, p. 85.

8 *Stat. Ire., 1-12 Edw. IV*, p. 353; *Stat. Ire., Hen. VI*, p. 191; *Cal. Carew MSS, 1515-75*, p. 423.

9 This document survived by chance among the records of the Blake family of Galway and is printed in *Blake family records*, pp 42-3; A.E. J. Went, 'Foreign Fishing

Fleets along the Irish coast' in *Cork Hist. Soc. Jn.*, liv (1949), pp 18-19, many other sixteenth century references are given in this study. Charles Smith, *The ancient and present state of the county and city of Cork*, 2 vols. (Cork, 1815), I, p. 281.

10 Cf. *Cal. Carew MSS, 1515-74*, p. 423; Charles Smith, *op. cit.*, II, p. 36. Domhnall O'Sullivan Beare in exile in 1605 wrote to Philip II of Spain, declaring 'that each year at least five hundred fishing boats came to his ports and by each of these he was paid a substantial sum of money'. Archivo General de Simancas MS E.1796.I am grateful to Micheline Kerney Walsh for this reference.

11 See D. B. Quinn and K. W. Nicholls 'Ireland in 1534' in *N.H.I.* III, p. 15n.; Childs & O'Neill 'Overseas Trade' p. 505; A proverb from the 'Noumbre of Weyghtes' — a fifteenth century commercial handbook, cited in *ibid.* p. 492; Carus-Wilson, *Overseas Trade of Bristol* pp 93, 161, 238, 243, 247, 264; Irish merchants were selling herring in Bristol in 1389, *Cal. close rolls, 1389-92*, p. 35.

12 *The Exchequer Rolls of Scotland (1264-1359)* eds. John Stuart and George Burnett (Edinburgh, 1878), p. 199; *Stat. Ire., Hen. VI*, pp 697 ff.

13 *Rot. pat. Hib.*, p. 130 no. 63; 'Pipe Roll of Cloyne' in *Cork. Hist. Soc. Jn.*, xix (1913), p. 60; A. E. J. Went, 'The Ling in Irish Commerce' in *R.S.A.I. Jn.*, lxxviii (1948), p. 119.

14 Cf. Hore, *Wexford town* II, *passim; Extents of Irish Monastic Possessions 1540-41* ed. N. B. White, (Dublin, 1943), p. 355; Longfield, *Anglo-Irish Trade* p. 48.

15 E. A. Lewis, 'The Development of Industry and Commerce in Wales during the Middle Ages' in *Trans. Royal Historical Soc.* (New series), xvii (1903), pp 150, 169n.; *Cal. close rolls, 1429-35*, p. 69.

16 See A. E. J. Went, 'Irish Monastic Fisheries' in *Cork. Hist. Soc. Jn.*, lx (1955), pp 47ff and a wealth of references in H. F. Hore, *And Enquiry into the legislation, control and improvement of the salmon and sea fisheries of Ireland*, (Dublin, 1850), *passim* also for Limerick see Robert Herbert 'The laxweir and fishers' stent of Limerick' in *N. Munster Antiq. Jn.*, V (1946-7), pp 49ff; *Irish Law Reports*, 1934, Pt I, pp 58-109.

17 *Ormond Deeds, 1350-1413*, nos 9, 17; M. J. Dodd, 'The manor and fishery of Killorglin' in *Galway Arch. Soc. Jn.*, xxi (1944), pp 140ff; A. E. J. Went, 'The Galway Fishery' in *R.I.A. Proc., xlix sect. C*, (1943-4), pp 187ff. Dublin Corporation had fisheries on the Liffey, see *R.S.A.I. Jn.*, lxxxiii (1953), pp 163ff; 'Monastic Fisheries' in *Cork. Hist. Soc. Jn.*, lx (1955) p. 51; Quinn *op. cit.*, p. 67.

18 Hore, *Wexford town*, V, p. 123; *Cal. pat. rolls, 1436-41*, p. 535; *ibid., 1446-52*, p. 28.

19 *Cal pat. rolls, 1399-1401*, p. 260, 403, 425; *ibid., 1401-5*, pp 31, 208, 209, 211, 376; *ibid., 1405-8*, pp 163, 170, 144, 433; *Cal. close rolls, 1402-5*, pp 408, 332; *ibid., 1405-9*, pp 208, 435; *ibid., 1409-13*, pp 32, 142, 143, 272; *ibid., 1413-19*, pp 4, 6, 11.

20 *Cal. pat. rolls, 1399-1401*, p. 260.

21 *Rot. pat. Hib.*, p. 131, no. 29.

22 Colin Platt, *Medieval Southampton A.D. 1000-1600* (London, 1973), p. 153; *Cal. pat. rolls, 1391-6*, p. 35 and *ibid., 1396-9*, p. 449; *Cal. close rolls, 1402-5*, p. 456.

23 N. J. G. Pounds 'The ports of Cornwall in the Middle Ages' in *Devon and Cornwall notes and queries*, xxiii (1947-9), p.72.

24 MacNeill, *op. cit.*, p. 139; *Rot. pat. Hib.*, p. 169, no. 22 and p. 172, no. 3; *ibid.*, p. 135, no. 162; *ibid.*, p. 189, no. 3 and p. 193, no. 162; Quinn, *loc. cit.*

25 Carus-Wilson, *Overseas Trade of Bristol*, p. 187; cf. customs accounts 1461 and 1479-80, pp 216-7, 219, 221, 228; Longfield, *Anglo-Irish trade*, p. 47.

26 In 1404 one barrel of salmon was included with fish which arrived in a ship of Rush — *Chester Customs*, p. 115; The monks of Llanthony, who owned estates in Co. Meath did ship salmon to England occasionally, presumably for their own needs cf. *Rot. pat. Hib.*, p. 130, no. 63; p. 135, no. 180.

27 *Ormond deeds* (1350-1413), p. 347, Iris Origo *The Merchant of Prato — Francesco de Marco Datini* (Middlesex, 1963), p. 286; *Cal. Carew MSS, Book of Howth*, p. 161; *R.I.A. Proc., LXXI (1961-2), Sect. C*, p. 196; 'Monastic Fisheries' in *Cork Hist. Soc. Jn.*, LX (1955), p. 49.

28 *The Register of John Swayne, Archbishop of Armagh, 1418-37*, ed. D. A. Chart (Belfast, 1935), p. 103 and p. 171.

29 A. E. J. Went, 'The Galway Fishery' in *R.I.A. Proc., xlix, sect. C*, (1943-4), p. 197; *Cal. doc. Ire., 1293-1301* p. 29, 'The Annals of Ireland 1443-68, translated from the Irish by Dudley Firbisse' ed. John O'Donovan in *Miscellany of Irish Archaeological Society* (Dublin, 1846), pp 234-5.

30 Carus-Wilson *op. cit.*, p. 259; *Rot. pat. Hib.*, p. 147, no. 237; National Library of Ireland, MS 2689, p.290; *The Red Book of Ormond* ed. N. B. White,(Dublin, 1932), p. 134; 'A Calendar of the Liber Albus and the Liber Niger of Christchurch Dublin', ed. H. J. Lawlor, in *R.I.A. Proc., XXVII sect. C*. (1907-9), p. 13.

The wine trade

1 Seamus Ó Néill, 'Early Maritime History of Ireland' in *Studies* XXXIV (1945), p. 410; *The History of Topography of Ireland*, trans. J. J. O'Meara (Mountrath, 1982), p. 122; M. D. O'Sullivan, 'Some Italian merchant bankers in Ireland in the later thirteenth century' in *R.S.A.I. Jn.*, lxxix (1949), p. 13.

2 Childs and O'Neill, 'Overseas Trade' p. 497 which uses the work of Jacques Bernard, in particular 'The Maritime Intercourse Between Bordeaux and Ireland *c.* 1450-*c.* 1520' in *Ir. Econ. & Soc. Hist.*, VII (1980), pp 7ff.

3 G. H. Orpen,. *Ireland under the Normans* 4 vols (Oxford, 1911) iv, p. 275; *ibid.*, p. 276; J. F.Lydon 'Ireland's participation' *passim*.

4 *P.R.I. Rep. D.K.* 37, p. 30, R.I.A. 12/D/11 p. 1; *Cal. doc. Ire., 1293-1301*, no. 626, R.I.A. 12/D/11 pp 2-6; *P.R.I. rep. D.K.* 37, p. 54; *ibid.*, p. 47; MacNiocaill, *Na Burgéisí*, ii, p. 513.

5 M. K. James *Studies in the Medieval Wine Trade*, ed. E. M. Veale (Oxford, 1971), pp 166-7; Patrick Daly, 'St. Thomas de Cantilupe and the process of canonization in the thirteenth and early fourteenth centuries', M.A. thesis, N.U.I. (U.C.D.) 1975, p. 185; *Cal. justic. rolls Ire., 1295-1303*, p. 298; *Rot. pat. Hib.*, p. 178, no. 67; *ibid.*, p. 188, no. 28, *ibid.*, p. 137, no. 223; *ibid.*, p. 136, no. 199; *ibid.*, p. 142, no. 237, *ibid.*, p. 198, no. 26.

6 *Cal. pat. rolls, 1364-77*, p. 19; L. F. Salzman, *English Trade in the Middle Ages* (London, 1964), p. 238; cf. Nicholls, *Gaelic and gaelicized Ireland*, p. 120; Maxwell, *Sources*, p. 375; for case of Thomas Mustard see above, p. 61; *Cal. justic. rolls Ire., 1305-7*, pp 25-27, 294, MacNiocaill, *Na Buirgéisí*, II, p. 511.

7 *Rot. pat. Hib.*, p. 86, no. 24; *Stat. Ire. John-Hen. V*, p. 477; *Rot. pat. Hib.*, p. 137, nos 223 and 226; *Chester Customs*, p. 112.

8 *Cal. pat. rolls, 1441-6*, p. 422; *ibid.*, *1452-61*, pp 60-61; *Chartularies of St Mary's*

Abbey, Dublin, II, p. xv; Carus-Wilson, *Overseas Trade of Bristol,* p 106-8, 'legge de Breon' may be Burrishoole in Mayo or perhaps *Lecc an Eich Bhuidhe,* Ballisodare Bay, Co. Sligo.

9 *Cal. pat. rolls, 1401-05,* p. 134; *ibid., 1399-1401,* p. 451, Carus-Wilson, *Overseas Trade of Bristol* p. 68, MacNiocaill, *Na Buirgéisí,* II, pp 508-9; *Stat. Ire., 12-22 Edw.IV,* p. 379.

10 Touchard, *op. cit.,* p. 238, cf. *Stat. Ire., 1-12 Edw IV,* p. 449; W. T. Johnston 'The English legislature and the Irish courts . . .' *Law Quarterly Review,* xl (1924), p. 94; E. A. Lewis 'A Contribution to the commercial history of medieval Wales' in *Y Cymmrodor* XXIV, (1913), pp 170-1.

11 James, *op. cit.,* pp 133-5; The *Patrick* was owned by Laurence Merryfeld, the master was Dermot Ballagh and Robert Broun of Waterford was the steersman. *Stat. Ire., Hen.VI,* p. 291; *Cal. close rolls, 1385-9,* p. 364; *ibid., 1339-41,* p. 624; *ibid., 1402-05,* p. 89.

12 *Cal. doc. Ire., 1293-1301,* no. 309; *Cal. justic. rolls Ire., 1305-07,* p. 40 and see Hore, *Wexford town,* I, p. 166.

13 *Cal. pat. rolls, 1441-6,* p. 422; *Rot. pat. Hib.,* p. 179, no. 21, his petition is in P.R.O., S.C. 8/113/5649; *Cal. pat. rolls, 1452-61,* pp 60-61; *ibid.* p. 347; *ibid.* 1313-17, p. 313; *Cal. justic. rolls Ire., 1305-07,* p. 354.

14 Cf. *Documents of the Affairs of Ireland before the King's Council,* ed.G. O. Sayles (I.M.C. Dublin, 1979), nos 159 and 174, *Cal. pat. rolls, 1327-30,* p. 84, *Ormond Deeds, 1350-1413,* pp 18-19. The earls of Ormond continued to collect prise until the beginning of the nineteenth century, see note in *Cork Hist. Soc. Jn. IX,* (1903), p. 129; *Cal. close rolls, 1381-5,* p. 347; *ibid., 1354-60,* p. 368. *ibid., 1402-05,* p. 89 — mentions unlawful prise taken from a Welsh ship sheltering in Waterford.

15 *Rot. pat. Hib.,* p. 63, no. 137, see also *Cal. close rolls, 1405-09,* p. 210; *Chester Customs,* p. 24n.; *Rot. pat. Hib.,* p. 209, no. 178; *Chester Customs,* p. 24.

16 *Cal. justic. rolls Ire., 1305-07,* p. 316, *Cal doc. Ire., 1302-07,* p. 134. Carnan has not been identified.

17 James, *op. cit.,* pp 142, 151ff. *P.R.I. rep. D.K.* 43, p. 60. Transport costs were fixed by the city authorities, MacNiocaill, *Na Buirgéisí,* II, p. 380.

18 *Cal. justic. rolls Ire., 1305-07,* p. 27; James *op. cit.,* p. 142. In 1309 a value of 56s. 8d. was put on a tun of wine in Dublin. R.I.A. 1A/53/29, f. 540, cf. earlier values 1A/53/27, f. 124 and f. 179; *Historical and Municipal Documents of Ireland, 1172-1320,* ed. J. T. Gilbert (London, 1870) p. xxxiv gives figures for butt or 1/2 tun.

19 H. L. Gray 'English foreign trade, 1446-1482' in *Studies in English trade in the fifteenth century,* ed. Power and Postan, p. 14, cf. Childs 'Ireland's trade', p. 18n.

20 R.I.A. 12/D/8, p. 383, cf. P.R.O.I. 1A/53/27, f. 208 (1306); *Account roll of Holy Trinity,* pp 109, 144. *Cal. doc. Ire., 1293-1301,* p. 164.

21 James *op. cit.,* p. 147; *Calendar of Papal Registers,* xiv, (1484-92), (London, 1960), p. 225. An act of Henry VIII for levelling dam-weirs provided a punishment for boatmen who used to tap casks of wine while transporting them up rivers, Hore 'An enquiry . . .' p. 4n.; *Blake Family Records,* p. 38; see above p. 82. Nicholls, 'Gaelic Society' p. 416.

22 *Rot. pat. Hib.,* p. 172, no. 3; *ibid.,* p. 169, no. 22; *Annals of Connacht, A.D. 1244-1544,* ed. A. M. Freeman (Dublin, 1944), p. 225; cf. *ibid.,* pp 451-3; see above [ ]; James Hardiman, *The History of the town and county of Galway* (Dublin, 1820.

repr. Galway, 1926, 1958), pp 63-4; Maxwell, *Sources*, pp 334-5, 375 n . The O'Neills did not always rely on trade to acquire wine. The Annals of the Four Masters recount that when Eoghan Ó Néill burnt the suburbs of Dundalk in 1444 he spared the town itself for 60 marks and 2 tuns of wine. Katherine Simms, 'Guesting and Feasting in Gaelic Ireland' in *R.S.A.I. Jn*, cxiii (1978), pp 67-100.

23 Transport costs — James *op. cit.*, pp 151-2; (1499) Carus-Wilson, *Overseas Trade of Bristol*, p. 112.

CHAPTER II

Wool production and marketing

1 *Cal. doc. Ire.*, *1252-84*, p. 195; cf. Geróid Mac Niocaill, *Na Manaigh Liatha in Éirinn*, *1142-c. 1600* (Dublin, 1959), p. 51n.

2 M. D. O'Sullivan, *Italian Merchant Bankers in Ireland in the Thirteenth century* (Dublin, 1962), Ch. VIII *passim*; Bolton, *English Economy*, p. 175; *ibid.*, p. 176; Kevin Down 'Colonial society and economy in the high middle ages' in *N.H.I.* II, pp 478-9.

3 P.R.O.I. 1A/53/27, f. 17; 1A/53/28, f. 290; 'Charters of the Abbey of Duiske' ed. J. H. Bernard and Constance Butler in *R.I.A. Proc.*, xxxv, sect. C. (1918), p. 124.

4 T. J. Westropp, 'Early Italian Maps of Ireland from 1300-1600 with notes on foreign settlers and trade' in *R.I.A. Proc.*, xxx, sect. C,. (1913), p. 380; J. H. A. Munro, *Wool, cloth and gold; the struggle for bullion in Anglo-Burgundian Trade*, *1340-1478* (Toronto, 1972), p. 2; *ibid.*, p. 3.

5 *Black Book of the Admiralty*, iv, p. 365. Conrad de Affleu, a German merchant shipped Welsh wool from Carmarthen twice in 1354 in the *Katherine* of Waterford. Cf. *Y Cymmorodor*, xxiv, p. 135; *Cal. close rolls*, *1337-9*, pp 419, 572; *ibid.*, p. 552; *ibid.*, *1341-3*, p. 72.

6 *Cal. pat. rolls*, *1354-8*, p. 405. Droup was an important figure having served in the wars in Ireland (*ibid.*, p. 377). He was appointed admiral of the king's fleet in Ireland in 1356. (*ibid.*, p. 431).

7 E. M. Carus-Wilson, 'The overseas trade of late Medieval Coventry' in *Economies et societes au moyen age; Melanges offerts a Edouard Perroy* (Paris, 1973), pp 373-4. The Chester accounts of the fourteenth and fifteenth century are not specific regarding varieties of goods but state so many horse loads or cart loads coming and going through the port; Carus-Wilson, *Overseas Trade of Bristol*, pp 253, 275-6; *Cal. close rolls*, *1364-8*, p. 25.

8 James Lydon, 'The expansion and consolidation of the colony, 1215-54' in *N.H.I.* II, p. 166.

9 Murage tolls on wool in Dublin and Waterford in MacNiocaill *Na Buirgéisí* II, p. 449 and cf. also the charter of New Ross in *ibid.*, I, p. 302; *Cal. justic. rolls Ire.*, *1305-7*, p. 2; James Lydon, 'Edward I, Ireland and Scotland' in Lydon, *Eng. and Ire.*, p. 55; Westropp, *loc. cit.*, *Select cases concerning the law merchant*, ed. Charles Gross & Hubert Hall (3 vols, London, 1908-32; Selden Society, xliii, xlvi, xlix), ii, pp 150-51.

10 *Cal. close rolls 1354-60*, p. 144; *ibid.*, *1339-41*, p. 591; *Cal. pat. rolls*, *1334-8*, p. 148 and see William O'Sullivan, *Economic History of Cork city from the earliest times to the Act of Union*, (Cork, 1937), p. 52; *Cal. close rolls*, *1337-9*, p. 78; *ibid.*, *1337-9*,

p. 78; *ibid.*, *1339-41*, p. 68 and see W. Stanford-Reid, 'Trade, Traders & Scottish Independence' in *Speculum*, xxix, (1954), pp 210ff.

11 Cf. Eileen Power, *The wool trade in English medieval history* (Oxford, 1941), p. 86; Bolton, *English Economy*, pp 193-4; William Goer entitled mayor of the staple of Waterford and distinguished from John Cotill mayor of the city — both witnessed a document in 1355, *Ormond Deeds, 1350-1413*, p. 15.

12 Cf. *Stat. Ire. John — Hen. VI*, p. 315, *Cal. pat. rolls, 1327-30*, p. 98.

13 Cf. *Documents on the affairs of Ireland before the King's Council*, ed. G. O. Sayles, no. 32; *Cal. pat. rolls, 1330-4*, p. 362; cf. Salzman, *English Trade in the Middle Ages*, p. 293 n.; *Cal. close rolls, 1354-60*, p. 260.

14 In 1375 the sheriffs of counties Kilkenny, Wexford, Waterford and Tipperary and the mayors etc. of Kilkenny, Thomastown, Ross, Wexford, Clonmel, Dungarvan and Cashel were warned regarding the observance of the staple at Waterford — *Rot. pat. Hib.*, p. 97, no. 259; *ibid.*, p. 92, no. 106; *ibid.*, p. 101, no. 57, also Hardiman, *The History of the town and county of Galway*, pp 58-9. It seems that several other staples were established in Ireland by royal officials, but these were declared illegal in 1380 — *Cal. close rolls, 1377-81*, p. 311.

15 *Rot. pat. Hib.*, p. 212, no. 92; *Cal. close rolls, 1392-6*, p. 246; *Cal. pat. rolls, 1416-22*, p. 42.

16 W. T. Johnston, 'The English Legislature and the Irish courts — the merchants of Waterford case, 1483' in *Law Quarterly Review*, xl, (1924), pp 100ff; In 1390 the citizens had been exempted from having to go to Calais — cf. *Cal. close rolls, 1389-92*, p. 211.

Cloth production and exports

1 Power, *The Wool Trade*, p. 102; O'Flaherty, *West Connaught*, appendix. *Arthur MS.*, p. 2.

2 Cf. Bolton, *English Economy*, pp 153ff; Origo, *The Merchant of Prato*, Ch. II *passim*; John Bradley, 'The Topography & Layout of medieval Drogheda' in — *Louth Arch. Soc. Jn.*, XIX, no. 2 (1978), p. 123; Carus-Wilson, *Overseas Trade of Bristol*, pp 248, 253, 256-7, 269-71; *Register of Wills*, ed. Berry, p. 8.

3 MacNiocaill, *Na Burgéisí*, II, pp 380, 383.

4 Carus-Wilson, *Overseas Trade of Bristol*, p. 180ff — the customs accounts for 1379, but note remarks of W.A. Childs in 'Ireland's Trade', p. 19; *ibid.*, p. 14; *The Oak Book of Southampton*, ed. Paul Studer, 3 vols. (Southampton Record Society, 1910-11), ii, p. 7. *Cal. of Public Records relating to Pembrokeshire*, ed. Henry Owen, 3 vols, (London, 1918), III, p. 220.

5 Carus-Wilson *op. cit.*, p. 170; *Cal. close rolls, 1327-30*, p. 175; MacNiocaill, *Na Buirgéisí*, II, p. 521; *Cal pat. rolls, 1377-81*, p. 281 — Regulations regarding widths and lenghts of cloth were often made cf. R.I.A. 24/H/17, p. 79; *Chester Customs*, p. 34 n. 5, p. 35 n. 3 and cloth exports to Chester from Ireland were considerable in the sixteenth century — *ibid.*, pp74ff.

6 Fazio degli Uberti, *Il Dittamondo e la Rime*, 2 vols (Bari, 1952); Charlemont, earl of, 'The Antiquity of the Woollen Manufacture in Ireland proved . . .' in *R.I.A. Trans.* I (1787), p. 18; *Cal. close rolls, 1381-5*, p. 55; Eileen Kane, 'Irish cloth in Avignon in the fifteenth century', in *R.S.A.I. Jn.*, cii (1972), p. 251n.

7 P. J. Lucas, 'Some words for Irish yarn and cloth in late Middle English' in

R.S.A.I. Jn., cvi (1976), p. 118. Cf. *Account roll of Holy Trinity*, p. 207. Childs and O'Neill, 'Overseas Trade', p. 503. These figures contradict the opinion of Conrad Gill, *The rise of the Irish Linen industry* (Oxford 1925; repr. 1964) which states (p. 6) that there was very little sale for Irish linen outside the country before 1500; *Local Port Books of Southampton*, vols I and II, ed. D. B. Quinn (Southampton Record Soc. 1937-8), II, p. 169; Eileen Kane, *op. cit.*, p. 249 and also in *R.S.A.I. Jn.*, cvii (1977), p. 143.

8 Nicholls 'Gaelic Society' p. 417 n ; *Blake Family Records*, p. 46; *ibid.*, p. 48, The will of John FitzHenry Blake of Galway (died 1468) mentions quantities of linen. O'Flaherty, *West Connaught*, p. 206.

9 R.I.A. 24/H/17, p. 77; *Register of wills*, ed. Berry, p. 16. Nicholls, *loc. cit.*, Longfield, *Anglo-Irish Trade*, pp 86ff.

10 H. F. McClintock, *Old Irish and Highland dress* (Dundalk, 1950), pp 96-102; *Anc. rec. Dublin*, p. 326; Many sixteenth century references in Maxwell, *Sources*, pp 347-51.

11 Cf. McClintock *op. cit.* and B. R. S. Megaw, 'The Irish Shaggy Mantle' in *Jn. of the Manx Museum*, V (1945-6), p. 175; *Cal. close rolls, 1336-81*, p. 38; *ibid.*, p. 156; *ibid.*, p. 145. In 1497 Irish cloth and mantles (*yersche mantels*) allowed into Bruges duty free — MacNiocaill, *Na Buirgéisí*, II, p. 521; see below p. 139 n.11.

12 *Cal. close rolls, 1396-9*, p. 161; N.L.I. MS 2689, n. 191.

13 Carus-Wilson, *Overseas Trade of Bristol*, pp 219, 221, 230, 239, 243, 256, 257,276, 280, 287 and Childs, 'Ireland's Trade', pp 14, 19; *Local Port Book of Southampton*, ii, p. 171; *Chester Customs*, pp 76, 80, 82; *Waterford Archives*, p. 318, regulations of 1493, *ibid.*, p. 326; *ibid.*, p. 373; MacNiocaill, *Na Buirgéisí*, ii, p. 383; Longfield, *Anglo-Irish Trade*, p. 77.

The importation of English cloth

1 Cited in *Studies in English trade in the fifteenth century*, ed. Power and Postan, p. 39; cf. Childs and O'Neill, 'Overseas Trade', p. 506, Childs 'Ireland's trade', pp 13, 17; In 1330 Augustine le Gayner shipped cloth and other goods from Dieppe to Cork, *Cal. close rolls, 1330-3*, p. 138.

2 Childs, *loc. cit.; Cal. pat. rolls, 1391-6*, p.594 — Blake was pardoned at the supplication of his kinsman 'the abbot of the Irishmen of Vienne in the Duchy of Daustry'(Vienna); Carus-Wilson, *Overseas Trade of Bristol*, p. 43; *ibid.*, p. 218; Childs, 'Ireland's trade', pp 22ff; *ibid.*, p. 21; Salzman, *English Trade in the Middle Ages*, pp 158-9.

3 Wilson, Port of Chester p. 91; R.I.A. 12/D/13, pp 134-5; Wilson, *op. cit.* p. 86; *Register of wills*, ed.Berry, pp 8-11; 15-18 also cf. Carus-Wilson 'The Overseas trade of late medieval Coventry', pp 372-3.

4 Wilson, *op cit.*, p. 90; *Facs. Nat. MSS Ire.*, III, 2, 39. In 1413 an Irishman Thomas Roche of Oxford, draper, was permitted to live in England despite the order for all Welsh and Irishmen to return to their homelands. *Cal. pat. rolls, 1413-16*, p. 122.

5 There are nine such letters of attorney between 1397-1424 in *Cal. pat. rolls; ibid., 1396-9*, pp 79, 531, *ibid., 1401-5*, pp 373, 395; *ibid., 1416-22*, p.236. Norton appointed attorneys in 1412, *ibid., 1408-13*, p. 391; *ibid., 1416-22*, p.303. Thomas Eyre, draper and John King, tailor, both of London, nominated attorneys in 1424, *ibid., 1422-9*, pp 199, 231; *Register of Wills*, ed.Berry, p. xix.

6 Wilson, Port of Chester, p.93; *Stat. Ire. 1-12 Ed IV*, pp 357ff; *Register of wills*, ed.Berry, p. 194. The Dublin merchants Guild of The Holy Trinity was established in 1451 by charter of Henry VI, see Charles Gross: *The Guild Merchant: A contribution to British municipal history*, 2 vols (Oxford, 1890), I, p. 134; R.I.A. 24/H/17, p. 77. Welles was owed 18d by Alice, wife of John Calff farmer and fisherman of Lusk, 1472. *Register of Wills*, ed. Berry, p. 52.

7 Cf. *Stat. Ire. 1-12 Ed IV*, p. 435; In addition to charters of Dublin, Drogheda, Waterford and Cork, see a Limerick charter of 1414 in Lenihan *op. cit.* pp 64-5 and one of Carrick-on-Suir (1366) in *Ormond Deeds 1350-1413*, pp 95-7; John D'Alton and J. R. O'Flanagan, *History of Dundalk and its environs* (Dublin, 1864), p. 70.

8 Wood, 'Commercial intercourse with Ireland', p. 266; Pole Hore MSS, vol VIII, pp 217-224; *Cal. justic. rolls Ire. 1295-1305*, p. 36; *ibid.*, p.463.

9 Wilson, 'Port of Chester' p.96; *Register of wills*, ed. Berry, p. 8; R.I.A. 24/H/17 p. 79;*Register of wills*, ed. Berry, p. 182.

10 N.L.I. MS 2689, no. 12; *A.U.* III, p. 209; cf. Agnes Conway *Henry VII's relationships with Scotland and Ireland 1485-98* (Cambridge, 1932), Appendix xii, p.174; Pole Hore MSS vol. ix, p. 366; *Arthur MS* pp 14-17; *Leabhar Branach* ed. Seán Mac Airt (Dublin, 1944), p. 215; *Facs nat. MSS Ire.*, iii, 2, no. V.

Trade in cow hides and calf skins

1 MacNiocaill, *Na Buirgéisí*, II, pp 523-533.

2 *Cal. close rolls, 1339-41*, p. 334.

3 *Cal. close rolls, 1369-74*, p. 169; Carus-Wilson, *Overseas Trade of Bristol*, p. 34; *ibid.*, p. 44.

4 *Cal. pat. rolls, 1429-36*, p. 540; Carus-Wilson, *Overseas Trade of Bristol*, 218ff; Power and Postan, *English Trade in the Fifteenth Century*, p. 187; Wilson, 'Port of Chester' pp 83-4; *The Black Book of the Admiralty*, I, p. 141.

5 J. F. Lydon, *Ireland in the Later Middle Ages*, p. 13;Childs and O'Neill, 'Overseas Trade', pp 495, 501; *Cal. close rolls, 1349-54*, p.578; *ibid., 1381-5*, p. 47; *Rot. pat. Hib.*, p. 212 no. 92; *Cal. pat. rolls, 1381-5*, p. 501; Exactly one hundred years later, in 1484 a dispute began between John Lawless of Drogheda and a Lisbon merchant over payment for a consignment of 400 hides Registrum Octaviani — No. 536.

6 *Cal. close rolls, 1339-41*, p. 591; *ibid., 1360-64*, pp 22-3.

7 *Cal. close rolls, 1377-81*, p. 150.

8 Kenneth Nicholls, *Gaelic and gaelicised Ireland in the Middle Ages* (Dublin 1972), p. 119; R.I.A. 12/D/12, pp 103-4.

9 Hore, *Wexford town*, I, pp 228-9;*Waterford Archives*, p. 306; *ibid.*, p. 318; *Galway Archives*, p. 396; *Waterford Archives*, p. 318.

10 Gearóid MacNiocaill, 'Socio-economic Problems of the Late Medieval Irish Town' in *The Town in Ireland (Historical Studies XIII)*, ed. D. Harkness and M. O'Dowd (Belfast, 1981), p. 18;*Ormond Deeds, 1350-1413*, p. 347;*Cal. Carew MSS. Book of Howth*, p. 358.

11 O'Flaherty, *West Connaught*, pp 198-210; *Arthur MS*, p. 14.

12 Henri Touchard, *Le Commerce maritime Breton a la fin du Moyen Age* (Paris, 1967), p. 238.

CHAPTER III

Salt and iron from Brittany and Spain

1 A. R. Bridbury, *England and the Salt Trade in the Later Middle Ages*, ch. IV; Bolton, *English Economy*, p. 169.

2 See above p. 104; *Cal. close rolls, 1385-9*, p. 329; *Cal. pat. rolls, 1408-13*, p. 474; *Rot. pat. Hib.*, p. 213, no. 142, p. 219, no. 50, cf. *Stat. Ire. 1-12 Edw IV*, p. 449; *Rot. pat. Hib.*, p. 256, no. 138.

3 R.I.A. 12/D/8, p. 423. Some iron came to Ireland from Normandy, cf. Mollat, *op. cit.*, p. 156; *Cal.pat. rolls, 1358-61*, p. 114; *Cal. close rolls, 1364-8*, p. 8. Waterford merchants got a similar permit.

4 R.I.A. 12/D/12, p. 133; cf. Platt, *Medieval Southampton*, pp 93-5, *Cal. close rolls, 1337-9*, p. 27; Carus-Wilson *Overseas Trade of Bristol*, p. 180 n and p. 181; *Cal. pat. rolls, 1377-81*, pp 77, 323. Cf. Bridbury, *op. cit.*, p. 125; *Cal. pat. rolls, 1429-36*, p. 199.

5 *Rot. pat. Hib.*, p. 257, nos 39, 68; Wilson, *Port of Chester*, p. 83; *English Trade in the fifteenth century*, ed. Power and Postan, pp 214ff; R.I.A. 12/D/8, p. 431.

6 *Rot pat. Hib.*, p. 257, no. 33, see also Carus-Wilson, *Overseas Trade of Bristol*, p. 63; *ibid.*, pp 106-8, see above p. 48; *ibid.*, (1461 a/c), p. 212ff; *ibid.*, pp 220, 222; *Rot pat. Hib.*, p. 257, no. 48.

7 *A. U.*, iii, (1379-1541), p. 311; *Register of wills*, ed. Berry, p. 83.

8 Salt for treating skins was brought from Galway to Athenry in 1401-2. *Rot. pat. Hib.*, p. 161, no. 55; *ibid.*, p. 172, no. 12, cf. also P.R.O. 14/53/27, f 51 where a warehouse with 80 carcases of beef and 94 hides is mentioned.

9 *Waterford Archives*, p. 319; Carcases were sent to England in 1378, (Carus-Wilson *Overseas Trade of Bristol*, p. 181) and in 1385-6, (*Rot. pat. Hib.*, p. 136, no. 200); Longfield, *Anglo-Irish Trade*, pp 105-7.

10 *Cal. close rolls, 1392-6*, p. 34; *Waterford Achives*, p. 296; MacNiocaill, *Na Buirgéisí*, ii, pp 487-90; *Register of wills*, ed. Berry pp 130-33 and *Na Buirgéisí*, ii, p. 380.

11 K.Down, 'Colonial society and economy', p. 464; O'Flaherty *West Connaught*, pp 198ff.

12 *Account roll of Holy Trinity*, pp 40-1; see the instructions regarding repairs to Dublin Castle in 1399, in P.R.O.I. 1A/53/30, f 25. Many examples from the 13th century in R. A. Stalley 'William of Prene and the Royal Works in Ireland' in *Jn. of the British Archaeological Assoc.*, cxxxi (1978), pp 30-49; *Cal. pat. rolls 1354-8*, p. 267.

13 Wilson, Port of Chester, p.83; *Cal. close rolls, 1392-6*, p. 353; Carus-Wilson, *Overseas Trade of Bristol*, pp 256, 258, 270, 271. Childs 'Ireland's Trade' p. 17. The Arthurs of Limerick had stocks of 'battery' — *Arthur MS* pp 3, 15; Childs, *op. cit.*, p. 20. The manufacture and import of pottery in medieval Ireland is discussed in McNeill, *Anglo-Norman Ulster*, pp 53-7.

14 *Register of wills*, ed. Berry, pp xxxi, 59, 48, MacNiocaill, *Na Buirgéisí*, ii, p. 487-9; *ibid.*, pp 392-3, *Anc. rec. Dublin*, I, p. 327.

15 *ibid; Stat. Ire. Hen. VI*, p. 83, J. F. Lydon 'Medieval Wateford' in *Decies*, XII (1979), pp 5-15. In 1495 the guild merchant in Limerick ordered every citizen with goods worth more than £20 to have weapons, including 'an English bow and sheaf of arrows'. Every freeholder to have a horse 'to assist the King' — Lenihan, *Limerick: its history and antiquities*, p. 697 n . In 1473 the 'Statute of Bows' required

merchants coming to Ireland to bring bows in proportion to the value of good imported e.g. £100 worth of goods — 100s. worth of bows. (*Stat. Ire. 12-21 Ed IV*, p. 99).

16 *Proc. King's council, Ire, 1392-3*, p. 160; *Waterford Archives*, p. 302; *ibid.*, p. 315; see above p. 34.

Millstones and building stone

1 R. O. Roberts 'The Mills of Anglesey' in *Trans. Anglesey Antiquarian Soc.* (1958), p. 5; Lewis, 'The Development of Industry and Commerce in Wales during the Middle Ages'; p. 144; R.I.A. 12/D/11, p. 11; P.R.O.I. 1A/53/23, p. 188; R.I.A. 12/D/8, p. 301; R.I.A 23/H/17, p. 49. These entries from the Memoranda Rolls abound in detail and list wages of smiths, carpenters, bricklayers etc. cf. J. F. Lydon, 'The Mills of Ardee in 1304', in *Louth Arch. Soc. Jn.*, XIX, 4 (1980), pp 259-63.

2 *Anc. rec. Dublin*, I, pp 327-8, cf. also p. 284.

3 D. M. Waterman 'Somersetshire and other foreign building stone in Medieval Ireland *c*. 1175-1400' in *Ulster Journal of Archaeology*, xxxiii (1970), p. 63; Some Caen stone from Normandy was also imported, cf. Canice Mooney 'Franciscan architecture in pre-Reformation Ireland' in *R.S.A.I. Jn.*, lxxvi (1956), pp 127 ff. Building stone consisting of 400 *libere petre* were sent by ship from Drogheda to Dublin for repairs to the castle in 1322-3, R.I.A. 12/D/13, p. 85; Waterman *op. cit.*, p.73; John Hunt and Peter Harbison 'Medieval English Alabasters in Ireland, in *Studies*, lxv (1976), pp 310-321. See also John Hunt, *Irish Medieval Figure Sculpture*, 2 vols, (Dublin and London 1974), *passim*. A link with Chester is suggested by a number of thirteenth century carved coffin lids in Co. Down. Cf. McNeill, *Anglo-Norman Ulster*, p. 45.

4 A. H. Dodd 'A History of Caernarvonshire 1284-1900' (Caernarvonshire History Soc., 1908), pp 35-6, there were local slate quarries in Ireland cf. *Ormond Deeds, 1172-1350*, p. 340; Hore, *Wexford town* iii, p. 202; P.R.O.I. 1A/53/30, f. 25.

CHAPTER IV

Luxury imports and miscellaneous exports

1 Cf. *Cal. close rolls 1429-35*, p. 276; Childs and O'Neill, 'Overseas Trade', p. 509; *P.R.I. rep. D.K.* 47, p. 58; *P.R.I. rep. D.K.* 43, p. 53; *Register of wills*, ed. Berry, p. 168.

2 O'Sullivan, *Italian Merchant Bankers*, p.109 n ; Catriona McLeod, 'Fifteenth century vestments in Waterford' in *R.S.A.I. Jn.*, lxxxii (1952), pp 85-98; Gearóid MacNiocaill, 'Register of St Saviour's Chantry, Waterford' in *Analecta Hibernica* 23, (1966), pp 148ff.

3 See my forthcoming article on the career of Lynch; Nicholls, 'Gaelic society and economy', p. 418; *Cal. Carew MSS, Book of Howth*, pp 357-9; *Registrum Iohannis Mey*, ed. W. G. H. Quigley and E. F. D. Roberts, (Belfast, 1972), pp 52, 432; *Anc. Rec. Dublin*, I, p. 349; R. J.Kelly 'Some old Galway Laws' in *R.S.A.I. Jn.*, XXV (1895), p. 383.

4 Childs, 'Ireland's Trade', p. 17; *Cal. pat. rolls, 1399-1401*, p. 451; *Stat. Ire. Hen. VI*, pp 236-7. Limerick man Martin Arthur had fourteen beehives in 1380 — his wife Gillian also kept bees. *Arthur MS* pp 2, 6.

5 *Cal. justic. rolls Ire.*, *1305-07*, p. 507; *Account roll of Holy Trinity*, pp XV; 100; *Ormond Deeds, 1350-1413*, p. 348; *The bardic poems of Tadh Dall Ó Huiginn*, ed. Eleanor Knott, 2 pts. (London, 1922, 1926), ii, p. 164.

6 Lydon, *Lordship*, pp 40-1; *Ormond Deeds, 1172-1350*, pp 111-12; *Account roll of Holy Trinity*, pp XV, 5. *Ormond Deeds, 1350-1413*, p. 348; Rev. Prof. Power 'On a find of ancient jars in Cork City' in *Cork Hist. Soc. Jn.*, XXIII (1928), p. 10.

7 Cf. Carus-Wilson, *Overseas Trade of Bristol*, pp 59, 232; *Cal. close rolls, 1377-81*, p. 24; Lydon, *loc. cit.*; Carus-Wilson, *Overseas Trade of Bristol*, pp 243, 265, 280; *ibid.*, pp 181, 211, 217, also Childs, 'Ireland's Trade', p. 20.

8 E. M. Veale, *The English Fur Trade in the later Middle Ages* (Oxford, 1966), p. 59; Hore, *Wexford town*, V, p. 218 n ; Wood, 'Commercial intercourse with Ireland', p. 263.

9 Veale, *op. cit.*, pp 169-70; *Cal. pat. rolls, 1391-6*, p. 729; *Rot. pat. Hib.*, p. 191, no. 84; *ibid.*, p. 213, no. 130; Childs and O'Neill, 'Overseas Trade', p. 492, Robin Frame says that the 4th earl of Ormond, the White Earl, was almost certainly the motivating force behind the Irish section of this poem — *English Lordship in Ireland*, p. 335.

10 Veale, *op. cit.*, pp 61, 169; Childs, 'Ireland's Trade', p. 14. Veale, *op. cit.*, p. 60; *Register of wills*, ed. Berry, pp 8-11, 15-18; Childs and O'Neill *op. cit.*, pp 500, 502; Childs 'Ireland's Trade', Table III, p. 19.

11 R. E. Glasscock, 'Land and People *c.*1300' in *N.H.I.*, II, p. 209; *Cal. Carew MSS Book of Howth*, p. 482; *Cal. justic. rolls. Ire.*, *1305-07*, p. 259; *ibid.*, p. 106, Hore, *Wexford town*, I, p.213; *Waterford Archives*, pp 299, 325; Bundles of firewood are also mentioned in 14th and 15th century wills of the Arthurs of Limerick — *Arthur MS*, pp 2, 7, 14.

12 Glasscock, *op. cit.*, p. 210. MacNiocaill, *Na Buirgéisí*, II, p. 388; *Rot. pat. Hib.*, p. 163, no.107; R.I.A. 12/D/12, p. 145; *ibid.*, p. 154; J. F. Lydon, 'Edward I, Ireland and the war in Scotland' in Lydon, *Eng. and Ire.*, pp 48-9; *Account roll of Holy Trinity*, pp 57, 60.

13 Wood, 'Commercial intercourse with Ireland', p. 252; Michel Mollat, *Le Commerce Maritime normand a la fin du Moyen Age*, (Paris, 1952), p.156. *Black Book of the Admiralty*, ii, p. 193; J. F. Lydon, 'The years of crisis 1254-1315', in *N.H.I.* II, p. 182; Childs, 'Ireland's Trade', p. 20; E. A. Lewis, 'The Development of Industry and Commerce in Wales during the Middle Ages' in *Trans. Royal Hist. Soc., New Ser.*, XVII (1903), p. 141; *A calendar of the Public Records relating to Pembrokeshire*, ed. Henry Owen, 3 vols (London, 1918), iii, p.173.

14 In the will of John Fitzhenry Blake, a merchant who died in Galway, in 1468, it is mentioned that one Odo O'Lensgy owed him 1,500 barrel staves (*tabullas dolorium*). O'Flaherty, *West Connaught*, p. 207.

15 J. P. Prendergast, 'Of hawks and hounds in Ireland', in *R.S.A.I. Jn., ii (1852), p.150; Cal. pat. rolls, 1374-7*, p. 393; *Rot. pat. Hib.*, p. 136, no. 190; *Stat. Ire. John-Hen. V*, p. 491; *Rot. pat. Hib.*, p. 147, no.236; *Cal. pat. rolls, 1391-6*, p. 409, *ibid., 1399-1401*, p. 239; *Rot. pat. Hib.*, p. 169, no. 19; *ibid.*, p. 171, no. 108.

16 *T.C.D. MS* 557, vi, pp 303-4; Childs, 'Ireland's trade', p. 20; *Stat. Ire. 12-22 Ed. IV*, p. 817. Prendergast, *op. cit.*, p. 150.

17 *Calendar of the Gormanstown Register*, ed. J. Mills and M. J. McEnery (Dublin, 1916), p. 14; P. H. Hore 'Extracts from the great Roll of the Irish Exchequer relating to Waterford and Ross 1273-1483' in *Cork Hist. Soc. Jn.*, XXIV, (1918), p. 22. The

afer was sometimes used as a baggage animal — *Account roll of Holy Trinity*, p. 211, *Rot. pat. Hib.*, p. 99, no. 282; Down, 'Colonial Society and economy', p. 474. The thirteenth century writer Walter of Henley pointed out that oxen were less expensive to feed, stronger on heavy land and could be eaten when their working life was over — Bolton, *English Economy*, p. 32; P. H. Hore *op. cit.*, p.21; J. F. Lydon, 'The years of Crisis, 1254-1315', in N.H.I. II, p. 198.

18 Richard Bennett and John Elton, *A History of Corn Milling IV — some feudal mills*, (1904, — re-issued Wakefield, 1975) p. 19n; Down, *op. cit.*, p. 478; P.R.O.I. 1A/53/29, f. 607; J. A. Watt 'Approaches to the history of fourteenth century Ireland' in *N.H.I., II, p. 309. Illustration in MS of Jean Creton (British Library, Harleian 1319).*

19 *P.R.O.I.1A/53/28, pp 425-8; Rot. pat. Hib.*, p. 71, no. 98; *ibid.*, p. 191, no. 89; E. M. Carus-Wilson, *Medieval Merchant Venturers* (London, 1967), p. 24; *Rot.pat. Hib.*, p. 266, no. 44; *ibid.*, p. 267, no. 40; Mollat, *op. cit.*, p. 156; State Papers, Milan, cited in Wood 'Commercial Intercourse with Ireland', p. 253.

20 *Cal. pat. rolls, 1374-7*, p. 13 — the provisions included 12 carcases of oxen and pigs; T.C.D. MS 557, vi, p. 13; Hore, *Wexford town*, II, p. 49; *Stat. Ire. 1-12 Ed IV*, p. 833; *Cal. pat. rolls, 1494-1509*, p. 577; *Stat. Ire. John-Hen. V*, pp 365, 499.

CHAPTER V

Types of trading and fishing vessel

1 Richard W. Unger, *The Ship in the Medieval Economy, 600-1600* (London and Montreal, 1980), Chapters 4 and 5. This wideranging study is based on the latest international technological and archaeological studies of medieval ships; Dorothy Burwash, *English merchant shipping 1460-1540* (Newton Abbot, 1969), p. 101; Platt, *Medieval Southampton*, p. 71; cf. Childs, 'Ireland's trade', p. 27.

2 Unger, *op. cit.*, pp 144, 222; *Cal. doc. Ire., 1293-1301*, no. 456; Burwash *op. cit.*, p. 135, Unger, *op. cit.*, p. 172; *Cal. close rolls, 1413-19*, p. 11; *Proc. King's council, Ire., 1392-3*, pp 72, 160; *ibid.*, p. 181.

3 Unger, *op. cit.*, p.172; John de Courcy-Ireland, 'Some notes on Wexford Maritime affairs in the Middle Ages and Renaissance' in *Jn. of Old Wexford Soc.*, iii (1970-1), p. 54; *Cal. pat. rolls, 1441-6*, p. 418, *ibid., 1461-7*, p.33; *Cal. close rolls, 1413-19*, p. 397; *The Oxford Companion to Ships and the sea*, ed. Peter Kemp (London 1976), p. 55; Unger, *op. cit.*, p.172.

4 Burwash, *op. cit.*, p. 96. Figures based on tonnages of merchant-ships hired by the king for military expeditions; *English trade in the fifteenth century* ed. Power and Postan, p. 240.

5 Unger, *op. cit.*, pp 216ff; *Cal. pat. rolls, 1429-36*, p. 199; *ibid., 1476-85*, p. 78; This map is reproduced as a frontispiece to vol II of *Cal. of State Papers relating to Ireland, 1509-1603*, (11 vols, London, 1860-1912); *Holinshead's Irish Chronicle 1577*, ed. Liam Miller and Eileen Power, (Dolmen Editions: 28, 1979), p. 234.

6 Unger, *op. cit.*, p. 212ff. Hore, *Wexford town*, I, p. 227. *Stat. Ire., Hen. VI*, p. 483.

7 Cf. Burwash, *op. cit.*, pp 120ff; *Cal. close rolls, 1405-09*, p. 208; *ibid., 1409-13*, p. 32; *Cal. pat. rolls, 1399-1401*, p. 260; *ibid., 1385-89*, p. 107; *ibid., 1334-38*, p. 569; *ibid., 1422-29*, p. 327 — mentions a ship of 140 tons to be arrested in Bristol to carry the goods of the earl of Ormond and stipulates that the earl is to pay for the use of the ship and the wages of the sailors.

145

8 Burwash, *op. cit.*, pp 126ff; *Rot. pat. Hib.*, p. 175, no. 124; *Stat.Ire. 1-12 Ed. IV*, p. 355; *Stat. Ire. 12-22 ED IV*, p. 387; D. B. Quinn, *Ulster 1460-1550*, pp 62-3; 'Shippes, piccardes, scaffes and lighters in and out unto the haven of the citie of Dyvelyn . . .' were taxed in 1483 — *Anc. recs. Dublin*, I, p. 364.

9 *Cal. doc. Ire., 1293-1301*, no.311; *ibid., 1171-1251*, nos 2244-5; *ibid.*, no. 2532, cf. also *P.R.I. Rep. D.K. 36*, p. 24; *Cal.doc. Ire.*, 1293-1301, no. 520. He had to repair the wall and give the king 15 hogsheads of wine; see above p. 54; *Rot. pat. Hib.*, p. 193, no. 184; *Waterford Archives*, p. 301;*Stat. Ire. 12-22 Ed. IV*, p. 571; *Galway Archives*, p. 396,*Waterford Archives* pp 302-3.

10 Cf. E. Scandurra, 'Medieval and Renaissance ships in Italy'. In *A History of Seafaring based on underwater archaelogy*, ed. G. F. Bass (London, 1972), pp 214-5 and for a different view see Unger, *op. cit.*, pp 24-5; cf. *Cal. justic. rolls Ire., 1295-1303*, pp 73, 126; cf. *Waterford Archives*, p. 299, *Galway Archives*, p. 394; cf. *Ormond deeds, 1350-1413*, p. 259.

11 The Italian trading companies on the other hand, did not normally own their own ships; they either chartered vessels from ship owners or paid carriage in ships which also carried other cargo. Origo; *Merchant of Prato*, p. 137; Lydon, 'Ireland's participation', pp 241, 258; Childs, 'Ireland's Trade', pp 227-30.

Navigation and sea-charts

1 Cf. E. G. R.Taylor, *The Haven-Finding Art — A history of Navigation from Odysseus to Captain Cook*, (London, 1971), Ch. V *passim*; T. J. Westropp, 'Early Italian maps of Ireland with notes on foreign settlers and trade'. In *R.I.A.Proc.* XXX, sect C, 1913, pp 361-428; *ibid.*, p. 362; M. C. Andrews 'The Map of Ireland A.D 1300-1700' in *Proc. Belfast Nat. Hist. Soc., 1922-3*, pp 14-15; Micheline Kerney Walsh has discovered A Survey of Irish ports and harbours in 1597 in Archivo general de Simancas, MS E 180.

2 *Sailing directions for the Circumnavigation of England and for a voyage to the straits of Gibraltar*, ed. James Gairdner (Hakluyt Soc. London, 1889); Burwash, *op. cit.*, p. 28; *Cal. close rolls, 1385-9*, p. 364.

3 *Sailing directions*, p. 19; cf. Childs and O'Neill, 'Overseas Trade' p. 521; P.R.O.I. 1A/53/27, f.213; *Cal. close rolls, 1381-5*, p. 72.

4 *Oak Book of Southampton*, p. 101, The king sometimes granted a wreck to a follower, e.g. William Herbert in 1465 was granted the gear, fittings and cargo of the *Gabriel* wrecked off the Irish coast. *Cal.pat. rolls, 1461-7*, p. 427; *ibid., 1334-8*, pp 147-8; *Cal. close rolls, 1339-1402*, p. 341; Hore, *Wexford town*, I, pp 251-4.

5 *Topography of Ireland*, p. 58; *Chartularies of St Mary's Abbey*, ii, p. 310; *Cal. close rolls, 1364-8*, pp 150-1; *Register of wills*, ed. Berry, p. xx.

6 *Black Book of the Admiralty*, iv, p. 61; *Chartularies of St Mary's Abbey* ii, p. xv; Robin Frame, *English Lordhship in Ireland*, p. 118.

7 Cf. *Chester Customs, 1404-5*, p. 103ff; Frame, *op. cit.*, p. 117; William Worcestre, *Itineraries*, ed. J. H. Harvey (Oxford, 1969), p. 171. Rosell was one of 16 merchants admitted to the Chester Guild Merchant in 1474-5 — Wilson, 'Port of Chester' p. 94. He was admitted to the franchise of Dublin in 1475 in right of his wife — *Anc. rec. Dublin*, I, p. 351.

8 *Itinerium Symonis Semeonis ab Hybernia ad Terram Sanctam*, ed. Mario Esposito (Dublin, 1960), pp 25-49.

Piracy off the Irish coasts

1 The Life of St Nectan, cited by N. J. G. Pounds 'The Ports of Cornwall in the middle ages'. In *Devon and Cornwall notes and queries*, xxiii (1947-9), p. 65; cf. *N.H.I.*, ix, pp 465-7.

2 Cf. W. Stanford-Reid 'Sea power in the Anglo-Scottish War 1296-1328'. In *The Mariner's Mirror*, xlvi (1960), pp 7, 16. J. F. Lydon, 'The impact of the Bruce invasion, 1315-27'. In *N.H.I.*, II, p. 153;*Cal. pat. rolls, 1317-21*, p. 313; *ibid.*, *1321-4*,p. 121;*ibid.*, p. 126.

3 R.I.A. 12/D/12, p. 87; R.I.A. 12/D/8, p. 385, the *Aliceot* would be a typical example of a merchant ship 'arrested for the king's service' for a certain period. This was a common occurrence in medieval times before the establishment of the Royal Navy. The owners were generally compensated for their services — in this case a new mast, three cables and 'a large rope for rigging' were supplied by the king when the ship was released from service. For details regarding arrest of ships, refitting, wages, etc. see Lydon, 'Edward I, Ireland and Scotland'. In Lydon, *Eng. and Ire.*, pp 47-50.

4 Stanford Reid, *op. cit.*, p. 23; Rot pat. Hib., p. 42, no. 17;*ibid.*, p. 49, no. 53; cf. *ibid.*, p. 201, no. 110; cf. The case of the *Flower of Minehead* (1482) in Carus-Wilson *Medieval Merchant Venturers*, pp 17-18.*Cal. close rolls, 1341-3*, p. . Cf. Michael Dolly 'Some Irish dimensions to Manx history'— an inaugural lecture published by Queens University, Belfast (1976).

5 *Rot. pat. Hib.*, p. 127, no. 243 and *ibid.*, p. 193, no. 184; cf. Art Cosgrove 'Ireland beyond the Pale, 1399-1460' in *N.H.I.* II, pp 574ff.

6 See above p. 40; T.C.D. MS 557, V, pp 270ff;*ibid.*, VI, pp 164 ff. Cf. Katherine Simms 'The King's Friend: O'Neill' in Lydon, *Eng. and Ire.*, p. 229. Registrum Octaviani (P.R.O.N.I.) no. 266. For these and other references in the Armagh registers I wish to thank Anthony Lynch, M.A. I am particularly grateful for the transcript of the examintion of James Ylane which he communicated to me by courtesy of Prof. J. A. Watt.

7 *Cal. of Papal Registers, 1427-47, pp 675-6; Cal. pat. rolls, 1441-6*, p.97; *ibid.*, p. 58; *ibid.*, p. 418, although this incident happened on 27 August 1437, the official 'letters of reprisal' were not issued until 28 May 1446; *Stat. Ire. Hen. VI*, pp 483 ff.

8 *Rot. pat. Hib.*, p. 201, no. 122 cf. Childs and O'Neill, 'Overseas Trade', p. 508, see above p.85. Registrum Octaviani, no. 537.

9 *The Annals of Ireland by Friar John Clyn*, p. 26 cf. R. G. Nicholson 'An Irish Expedition to Scotland in 1335'. In *Irish Historical Studies*, xiii (1962-3), pp 197ff; *Rot. pat. Hib.*, p. 127, no. 243; *Cal. pat. rolls, 1413-16*, p. 241; *Stat. Ire. Hen. VI*, p. 317, *The Annals of Ireland 1443-68* . . . by Dudley Firbissse, p. 236, *Stat. Ire. Hen VI*, pp 311, 671.

10 *Stat. Ire., 1-12 Ed IV*, p. 467; R.I.A. 24/H/17, pp 211-217. Lewis, 'The Development of Industry and Commerce in Wales during the Middle Ages'. p. 171; See above p. 110.

11 *Cal. close rolls, 1354-60*, p. 276, *ibid.*, p. 367. Reprisals and the arrest of citizens of Castro Urdiales took place in London in 1357 but these were left off as an enquiry failed to establish exactly what happened. Cf. MacNiocaill, *Na Buirgéisí*, ii, pp 509 ff; *Rot. pat. Hib.*, p. 101, no. 46; *Cal. close rolls 1377-81*, p. 24;*The Council Book of Kinsale* ed. Richard Caulfield, p. xi; *Rot. pat. Hib.*, p. 114, nos 193-4.

12 *Rot. pat. Hib.*, p. 114, no. 196; *P.R.I. Rep. D.K.* 55, p. 118; *Cal. Carew MSS, Book of Howth*, pp 470-1; *A.U.*, iii (1379-1541), p. 33, Hardiman, *Galway*, pp 51-2; *Cal. pat. rolls, 1399-1400*, p. 254. The Aran Is. and Galway city have sometimes been confused with Arran Is. and Galloway in Scotland. Hardiman mentions the expedition of 1335 (no. 9 above) as going to the Aran Is!

13 Lenihan, *Limerick*, p. 70, cf. Unger *op. cit.*, p. 210; *Cal. pat. rolls 1399-1401*, p. 451; Lenihan, *op. cit.*, p. 367 n — citing manuscripts of the Arthur family.

14 Carus-Wilson, *Medieval Merchant Venturers*, p. 15; *The Little Red Book of Bristol*, ed. F. B. Bickley, 2 vols (Bristol, 1900), ii, p. 232; *Cal. pat rolls, 1452-61*, p. 60 and the sequel is related in Carus-Wilson *Overseas trade of Bristol*, p. 93; *Cal. pat. rolls, 1476-85*, p. 79; *The Council Book of Kinsale*, p. xiv.

I thank Philomena Connolly for references above in the class of Ancient Petitions, SC8, P.R.O. London.

Bibliography

I MANUSCRIPT SOURCES

National Library of Ireland, MS 2689, Canon Leslie Collection: Typescript copy of Bishop Reeve's Calendar of Primate Prene's Register (1430-1476).

Public Record Office of Ireland. 1A/49/133-135. J. F. Ferguson collection of extracts and notes from the Memoranda rolls Edward 1-Henry VIII.

—— 1A/49/146-149. J. F. Ferguson repertory to the Memoranda rolls Edward III to Henry VII.

—— 1A/53/27-28, 30. P.R.O.I. Calendar of Memoranda rolls.

Public Record Office of Northern Ireland. Registrum Octaviani.

Royal Irish Academy. 12/D/8, 11-14; 23/H/17. J. F. Ferguson collection of extracts from the Memoranda rolls.

Trinity College, Dublin. MS 577. Bishop Reeve's transcript of the Register of Archbishop Prene.

St. Peter's College, Wexford. The P. H. Hore Collection relating to the history of Wexford town and county.

II PRINTED SOURCES

Account roll of the priory of the Holy Trinity, Dublin, 1337-1346. Ed. James Mills, R.S.A.I., Dublin 1891.

*Annála Connacht: the Annals of Connacht, A.D. 1224-1544. Ed.*A. M. Freeman. Dublin, 1944.

The Annals of Ireland by Friar John Clyn and Thady Dowling, together with the annals of Ross. Ed. Richard Butler. Dublin, 1849.

Annals of Ireland, 1443-1468, translated from the Irish by Dudley Firbisse. *Ed.* John O'Donovan. In *Miscellany of Irish Archeological Society*, Vol. i, Dublin, 1846, pp 258-9.

Annála ríogachta Éireann: Annals of the kingdom of Ireland by the Four Masters from the earliest period to the year 1616. Ed. and *trans.* John O'Donovan. 7 vols. Dublin, 1851; reprint New York, 1966.

The Annals of Loch Cé: a chronicle of Irish affairs 1014-1590. Ed. W. M. Hennessy, 2 vols, London, 1871; reflex facsimile I.M.C., Dublin, 1939.

*Annála Uladh, Annals of Ulster, a chronicle of Irish affairs 431-1131, 1155-1541. Ed.*W. M. Hennessy and Bartholomew MacCarthy. 4 Vols, Dublin, 1887-1901.

Archives of the municipal corporation of Waterford. *Ed.* J. T. Gilbert. In *H.M.C. rep. 10, app. v (1885)*, pp 265-339.

149

Archives of the town of Galway. *Ed.*J. T.Gilbert. In *H.M.C. rep. 10, app. v (1885)*, pp 380-520.

The Arthur Manuscript. *Ed.* E. A. MacLysaght and John Ainsworth. In *N. Munster Antiq. Jn.*, 8 (1958), pp 3-19.

The Bardic Poems of Tadhg Dall Ó Huiginn. Ed. Eleanor Knott. 2 pts. London, 1922, 1926.

The Black Book of the Admiralty. Ed. Sir Travers Twiss. 4 vols. London, 1871-76.

Blake Family Records, 1st series, 1300-1599. Ed. M. J. Blake.London, 1902.

Calendar of ancient records of Dublin, in the possession of the Municipal Corporation of that city. I, *Ed.* J. T. Gilbert. Dublin, 1889.

Calendar of the Carew manuscripts preserved in the archepiscopal library at Lambeth, 1515-1634. 6 vols. London, 1867-73.

Calendar of the close rolls preserved in the Public Record Office Edward II to Henry VII, 1307-1509. 42 vols. London, 1892-1963.

Calendar of documents relating to Ireland in the Public Record Office, London. Ed. H. S. Sweetman. 5 vols. London, 1875-86.

Calendar of entries in the Papal registers relating to Great Britain and Ireland: Papal letters, vol. viii A.D. 1427-1447; Vol. xiv A.D. 1484-1492. London, 1909; 1960.

Calendar of the Gormanston Register. Ed. James Mills and N.J. McEnery. R.S.A.I., Dublin, 1916.

Calendar of the justiciary rolls or proceedings in the court of the Justiciar of Ireland preserved in the Public Record Office of Ireland, xxiii Edward I to vii Edward II, 1295-1314, 3 vols. Dublin, 1905-1956.

A Calendar of the Liber Niger and the Liber Albus of Christchurch, Dublin. *Ed.* H. J. Lawlor. In *R.I.A Proc.*, xxvii (1907-9), C. pp 1-93.

Calendar of Ormond Deeds, vols. 1-IV, (1172-1547). Ed. Edmund Curtis, I.M.C., Dublin, 1933-7.

Calendar of the patent rolls preserved in the Public Records Office, Edward II to Henry VII, 1307-1509 44 Vols. London, 1894-1916.

Calendar of the Public Records relating to Pembrokeshire. Ed. Henry Owen. 3 Vols. London, 1918.

Catalogue of the pipe rolls of the Irish Exchequer in the *35th-39th, 42nd-45th, 47th, 53rd and 45th Reports of the Deputy Keeper of the Public Records of Ireland.*

The Census of Ireland for 1851 Pt. V, Vol. i, (Tables of deaths).

'Charters of the Abbey of Duiske' *Eds.* J. H. Bernard and Constance Butler. In *R.I.A.Proc.*, xxxv (1918), C, pp 124ff.

Chartularies of St Mary's Abbey, Dublin with the register of its house at Dunbrody and Annals of Ireland. Ed. J. T. Gilbert. 2 Vols. London, 1884.

Chester Customs Accounts 1301-1566. Ed. K. P. Wilson, Liverpool, 1969.

The Council Book of Kinsale. Ed. Richard Caulfield. Guildford, 1878.

Court of Exchequer records relating to Kerry. *Ed.* Anon. in *Kerry Arch. Mag.*, iv (1917), pp 124-146.

Documents on the Affairs of Ireland before the Kings Council. Ed. G. O. Sayles I.M.C. Dublin, 1979.

The Exchequer Rolls of Scotland, Vol. i, (1264-1359). *Ed.* John Stuart and George Burnett. Edinburgh, 1878.

150

Extents of Irish Monastic Possessions, 1540-1541. Ed. N. B. White, I.M.C., Dublin, 1943.

Facsimiles of the national manuscripts of Ireland. Ed. J. T. Gilbert. 4 vols. Dublin, 1874-84.

Expugnatio Hibernica: The conquest of Ireland by Giraldus Cambrensis. Ed. A. E. Scott and F. X. Martin. R.I.A., Dublin, 1978.

Giraldus Cambrensis, *The History and Topography of Ireland.* The first version. *Trans.* J. J. O'Meara. Mountrath, 1982.

Historical and Municipal documents of Ireland, 1172-1320. Ed. J. T. Gilbert. London, 1870.

Holinshead's Irish Chronicle, 1577. Ed. Liam Miller and Eileen Power. Dolmen editions: 28, 1979.

Itinerium Symonis Semeonis ab Hybernia ad Terram Sanctam. Ed. Mario Esposito, Dublin, 1960.

Leabhar Branach: The Book of the O'Byrnes.Ed. Sean MacAirt. Dublin, 1944.

The Libelle of Englyshe Polycye, a poem on the use of sea power 1436.Ed. Sir George Warner. Oxford, 1926.

The Little Red Book of Bristol. Ed. F. B. Bickley. 2 Vols, Bristol, 1900.

Local Port Book of Southampton for 1439-40. Ed. H. S. Cobb. Southampton Record Series, 1961.

*The Oak Book of Southampton of c. A.D 1300. Ed.*Paul Studer. 3 Vols, Southampton Record Society, 1910-11.

The Overseas trade of Bristol in the later middle ages. Documents selected and edited by E. M. Carus-Wilson. Bristol, 1939. reprint 1967.

The pipe roll of Cloyne, *Ed.* Caulfield, O'Riordan, Coleman and Berry. In *Cork Hist. Soc. Jn.,* xix (1913), pp 53-61; 116-125; 157-167. xx (1914), pp 42-56, 85-108; 124-139.

The Port Books or Local Customs accounts of Southampton for the reign of Edward IV. Ed. D. B. Quinn and A. Ruddock. 2 vols, Southampton Record Society, 1937-8.

The Red Book of Ormond.Ed. N. B. White. I.M.C., Dublin, 1932.

The Register of John Swayne, Archbishop of Armagh, 1418-1439. Ed. D. A. Chart. H.M.S.O., Belfast, 1935.

Register of St Saviour's Chantry, Waterford. *Ed.* Gearóid Mac Niocaill. In *Analecta Hibernica,* 23 (1966) pp 135-222.

Register of the wills and inventories of the diocese of Dublin in the time of archbishops Tregury and Walton 1457-1483. Ed. H. F. Berry. R.S.A.I., Dublin, 1898.

Registrum Iohannis Mey. Ed. W. G. H. Quigley and E. F. D. Roberts, Belfast, 1972.

A Roll of the Proceeding of the Kings Council in Ireland, 16th Richard II, 1392-93. Ed. James Graves. London, 1877.

Rotulorum Patentium et Clausorum Cancellariae Hiberniae Calendarium. Ed. Edward Tresham. Dublin, 1828.

Sailing Directions for the Circumnavigation of England and for a voyage to the Straits of Gibraltar from a fifteenth century manuscript. Ed. James Gairdner. Hakluyt Soc., London, 1889.

151

Select cases concerning the Law merchant. Ed. C. Gross and H. Hall. Selden Society Publications xlvi, (1929), Appendix 3.

Select cases in Chancery, 1364-1471. *Ed.* W. P. Buildon. Selden Society, 1896.

Statutes, Ordinances, Acts of Parliament of Ireland, John to Henry V. Ed. H. F. Berry. Dublin, 1907.

The Statute rolls of the Parliament of Ireland, Reign of Henry the Sixth. Ed. H. F. Berry. Dublin, 1910.

The Statute rolls of the Parliament of Ireland, First to the Twelfth years of the Reign of King Edward the Fourth.Ed. H. F. Berry. Dublin, 1914.

The Statute Rolls of the Parliament of Ireland, Twelfth and Thirteenth to the Twenty-first and Twenty-second years of the Reign of Edward the Fourth. Ed. J. F. Morrissey. Dublin, 1939.

Ulster and other Irish Maps c. 1600. Ed. G.A. Hayes-McCoy. I.M.C. Dublin, 1964.

William Worcestre: *Itineraries. Ed.* John H. Harvey. Oxford, 1969.

III SECONDARY WORKS

Andrews, M. C. 'The map of Ireland A.D. 1300-1700'. In *Belfast Natur. His. Soc. Proc.,* (1922-3) pp 9-32.

Asplin, P. W. A. *Medieval Ireland c. 1170-1495:* a bibliography of secondary works. R.I.A., Dublin, 1971.

Bagley, J. J. *Historical Interpretation: The Sources of English medieval history 1066-1540.* Middlesex, 1965.

Beardwood, Alice. *Alien merchants in England, 1350-1377, their legal and economic position.* Cambridge, (Mass.) 1931.

Bennett, Richard & Elton, John. *A History of Corn Milling* IV, *Some feudal Mills.* (1904) New ed. Wakefield, 1975.

Bernard, Jacques, 'The Maritime Intercourse between Bordeaux and Ireland *c.* 1450-*c.* 1520'. In *Ir. Econ. & Soc. Hist.,* VII. (1980), pp 7-21.

Bolton, J. L. *The Medieval English Economy: 1150-1500.* London, 1980 (Reprint with supplement, 1985).

Bradley, John 'The topography and Layout of Medieval Drogheda'. In *Louth Arch. and Hist. Jn.,* XIX No. 2 (1978), pp 98-127.

Braudel, Fernand. *Civilisation and Capitalism, 15th-18th Century.* 2 vols. London, 1981, 1985.

Bridbury, A. R. *England and the Salt Trade in the later Middle Ages.* Oxford, 1955.

Brooks, Eric St John. 'Fourteenth century monastic estates in Meath: the Llanthony cells of Duleek and Colp'. In *R.S.A.I. Jn.,* lxxxiii (1953), pp 140-9.

Burwash, Dorothy. *English Merchant Shipping, 1460-1540.* Newton Abbot, 1969.

Butler, W. F. T. 'Town life in medieval Ireland'. In *Cork Hist. Soc. Jn.,* vii (1901), pp 17-25; 80-90; 205-215.

Cambridge economic history of Europe. Vol. ii-iii, Cambridge, 1952, 1965. *Vol. II (1952): Trade and industry in the middle ages; III (1965) Economic organisation and policies in the middle ages.*

Carus-Wilson, E.M. *Medieval Merchant Venturers.* London, 1967.

—— 'The oversea trade of lated medieval Coventry' In *Economies et societes au moyen age: Melanges offerts a Edouard Perroy.* Paris, 1973.

—— and Coleman, O, *England's Export trade, 1275-1547.* Oxford, 1963.

Chart, D. A. *An Economic history of Ireland.* Dublin, 1920.

Charlemont, earl of 'The antiquity of the woollen manufacture in Ireland proved from a passage . . .'. In *R.I.A. Trans.*, i, (1787), sect 3, pp 17-24.

Childs, W. A. 'Ireland's trade with England in the later Middle Ages'. In *II. Econ. & Soc. Hist.* IX (1982), pp 5-33.

—— & Timothy O'Neill. 'Overseas Trade'. In *N.H.I.*, II, pp 492-524.

Coleman, James. 'The bickerings between the citizens of Waterford and the O'Driscolls of Baltimore in the 14th, 15th and 16th centuries'. In *Waterford Archaeological Society Jn.*, xiii, (1909), pp 1-6.

Connolly, Philomena.'The Irish memoranda Rolls — some unexplored aspects'. In *Ir. Econ. & Soc. Hist.*, III (1976), pp 66-74.

Conway, Agnes. *Henry VII's relations with Scotland and Ireland, 1485-1498.* Cambridge, 1932.

Cortisao,A. 'The North Atlantic nautical chart of 1424'. In *Imago Mundi*, x (1953),pp 2-14.

Cosgrove, Art. *Late Medieval Ireland, 1370-1541.* Dublin, 1981.

—— 'Ireland beyond the Pale: 1399-1460'. In *N.H.I.*, II, pp 569-590.

Cullen, L. M. *Life in Ireland*, London, 1968.

Curtis, Edmund. *A Hstory of Medieval Ireland.* London, 1938. reprint 1968.

—— 'Janico Dartas, Richard II's 'Gascon squire' his career in Ireland, 1394-1426.' in R.S.A.I. Jn., lxiii (1933), pp 182-205.

—— 'Rental of the manor of Lisronagh 1333 and notes on betagh tenure in medieval Ireland.' In *R.I.A. Proc.*, xliii, sec. C (1934-5), pp 41-76.

—— 'The sheriffs account of the Honour of Dungarvan, of Tweskard in Ulster and of county Waterford, 1261-1263'. In *R.I.A. Proc.*, xxxix, sect c, (1929-31), pp 1-17.

D'alton, John. *History of Drogheda*, 2 vols, Dublin, 1844.

—— O'Flanaghan, J.R. *History of Dundalk and its environs*, Dublin, 1864.

Daly, Patrick. 'St Thomas de Cantilupe and the process of canonization in the thirteenth and early fourteenth centuries'. (M.A. Thesis, N.U.I. (U.C.D.) 1975).

Davies, D. J. *The Economic history of South Wales prior to 1800. Cardiff, 1933.*

De Courcy-Ireland, John, *Ireland and the Irish in Maritime History.* Dublin, 1986.

—— 'Some notes on Wexford maritime affairs in the middle ages and the renaissance' in *Jn. Old Wexford Society*, iii (1970-1) pp 50-55.

Dodd, A. H. *A History of Caernarvonshire 1284-1900.* Caernarvonshire Historical Society, 1908.

Dodd, M. J. 'The manor and fishery of Killorglin, Co. Kerry'. In *Galway Arch. Soc. Jn.*, xxi (1944), pp 140-173.

Dolley, Michael. *Anglo-Norman Ireland.* Dublin, 1972.

—— *Medieval Anglo-Irish Coins.* London, 1972.

Down, Kevin. 'Colonial Society and Economy in the High Middle Ages'. In *N.H.I.*, II, pp 439-81.

BIBLIOGRAPHY

Edwards, R. D. 'The beginning of municipal government in Dublin'. In *Dublin Historical Record.* i (1938), pp 2-18.

Ellis, S. G. 'Irish Customs Administration under the early Tudors'. In *I.H.S.*, XII (1980-1), pp 271-7.

Empey, C. A. 'The Butler lordship; in *Jn. of the Butler Society*, iii (1970-71), pp 174-187.

—— 'Conquest and Settlement: Patterns of Anglo-Norman Settlement in North Munster and South Leinster'. In *Ir. Econ. & Soc. Hist.*, XIII (1986), pp 5-31.

Frame, Robin. *English Lordship in Ireland: 1318-1361.* Oxford, 1982.

Gill, Conrad, *The Rise of the Irish Linen Industry*, Oxford, 1925. Reprint 1964.

Glasscock, R. E. 'Land and People *c.* 1300'. In *N.H.I.*, II, pp 205-239.

Grant, I. F. *The Economic History of Scotland*, London, 1934.

Gras, N. S. B. *The early English customs system.* Cambridge (Mass.), 1915.

Green, A. S. *The making of Ireland and its undoing.* London, 1908.

—— *Town life in the Fifteenth Century.* 2 Vols. London, 1894.

Gross, Charles. *The Guild Merchant: A contribution to British municipal history.* 2 vols. Oxford, 1890.

Gwynn, Aubrey. 'The Black Death in Ireland'. In *Studies*, xxxiv (1935), pp 25-42.

—— 'Medieval Bristol and Dublin'. In *I.H.S.*, v (1946-7), pp 275-86.

—— *The Medieval Province of Armagh, 1430-1645.* Dundalk, 1946.

—— and Hadcock, R. N. *Medieval Religious Houses: Ireland.* London, 1970.

Hardiman, James. *The History of the town and county of Galway.* Dublin, 1820. reprint, Galway, 1926, 1958.

Herbert, Robert. 'The laxweir and fishers stent of Limerick. In *N. Munster. Antiq. Jn.*, v. (1946-7), pp 49-61.

Hore, H. F. *An enquiry into the legislation, control and improvement of the salmon and sea fisheries of Ireland.* London, 1850.

Hore, Herbert and Graves, James. *The Social state of the southern and eastern counties of Ireland in the sixteenth century.* Dublin, 1870.

Hore, P. H. 'Extracts from the great roll of the Irish Exchequer relating to Waterford and Ross, 1293-1483'. In *Cork Hist. Soc. Jn.*, xxiv (1918), pp 16-28.

—— *History of the town and county of Wexford*, 5 vols. London, 1900-06.

Hunt, John. *Irish Medieval Figure Sculpture: 1200-1600.* 2 vols. Dublin & London, 1972.

—— and Harbison, Peter, 'Medieval English alabasters in Ireland'.In *Studies*, lxv (1976), pp 310-321.

James, M. K. *Studies in the medieval wine trade.* ed. E. M. Veale, Oxford, 1971.

Jones, G. P. 'Trading in medieval Caernarvon'. In *Trans. Caernarvonshire Historical Society*, x (1949), pp 3-12.

Johnston, W. J. 'The English legislature and the Irish courts — the merchants of Waterford Case, 1483'. In *Law Quarterly Review*, xl (1924), pp 91-106.

Kane, E. M. C. 'Irish cloth in Avignon in the fifteenth century'. In *R.S.A.I. Jn.*, cii (1972), pp 24-5.

—— 'More about Irish cloth in Avignon in the fifteenth century'.In *R.S.A.I. Jn.*, cvii (1977), p. 143.

Kelly, R. J. 'Some old Galway laws'. In *R.S.A.I. Jn.*, xxv (1895), pp 382-4.

Kemp, Peter (ed.) *The Oxford Companion to Ships and the Sea*, London, 1976.

Kershaw, Ian. 'The great famine and agrarian crisis in England, 1315-1322'. In *Past and Present*, lix (1973), pp 3-50.

Lanstrom, Bjorn.*Sailing Ships*. London, 1969.

Lenihan, Maurice. *Limerick: its history and antiquities*. Dublin, 1866.

Lewis, E. A. 'A contribution to the commercial history of medieval Wales, with tabulated accounts from 1301-1547'. In *Y Cymmrodor*, xxiv (1913), pp 86-187.

――― 'The development of industry and commerce in Wales during the middle ages' in *Royal Historical Society Transactions, xvii New Series (1903), pp 121-174.*

--- *The medieval boroughs of Snowdonia*. London, 1912.

Longfield, A. K. *Anglo-Irish trade in the sixteenth century*. London, 1929.

Lucas, A. T. 'Cattle in ancient and medieval Irish Society'. In *O'Connell School Union Record* 1937-58 (1958), pp 75-85.

Lucas, P. J. 'Some words for Irish yarn and cloth in late Middle English'. In *R.S.A.I. Jn.*, cvi (1976), pp 118-9.

Lydon, J. F.*The Lordship of Ireland in the middle ages*. Dublin, 1972.

――― *Ireland in the later middle ages*. Dublin, 1973.

――― 'Edward I, Ireland the war in Scotland, 1303-1304'. In Lydon, *Eng. and Ire.*, pp 43-64.

――― 'The expansion and Consolidation of the Colony: 1216-54'. In *N.H.I.*, II, pp 156-78.

――― 'The years of crisis 1234-1315'. In *N.H.I.* II, p. 179-204.

――― 'The Impact of the Bruce Invasion, 1315-27'. In *N.H.I.*, II, pp 275-302.

――― Ireland's participation in the military activities of English kings in the thirteenth and early fourteenth centuries. (Ph.D. thesis, University of London, 1955).

――― 'Medieval Waterford'. In *Decies* 12 (1979), pp 5-15.

――― 'The mills of Ardee in 1304'. In *Louth Arch. and Hist. Jn.*, XIX (1980), pp 259-263.

――― 'Survey of the memoranda rolls of the Irish Exchequer, 1294-1509'. In *Anal. Hib.*, xxiii (1966), pp 51-134.

Mace, F. A. 'Devonshire ports in the fourteenth and fifteenth centuries' in *Royal Historical Society transactions*, vii, 4th series, (1925), pp 98-126.

McEnery, M. J. 'The state of agriculture and the standard of living in Ireland 1240-1350'. In *R.S.A.I. Jn.*, L (1920), pp 1-18.

McClintock, H. F. *Old Irish and Highland Dress*, Dundalk, 1950.

MacLeod, Catriona. 'Fifteenth century vestments in Waterford'. In *R.S.A.I. Jn.*, lxxxii (1952), pp 85-98.

MacLysaght, Edward. 'Documents relating to the wardenship of Galway'. In *Anal. Hib.*, xiv (1944), pp 1-249.

MacNeill, Charles. 'Some Drogheda guilds and properties;. In *Louth Arch. Soc. Jn.*, vi, no. 4 (1928) pp 239-246.

MacNeill, T.E. *Anglo-Norman Ulster: The History and Archaeology of an Irish Barony 1177-1400*, Edinburgh, 1980.

Mac Niocaill, Gearóid. *Na Buirgéisí, XXII-XV aois*. 1 vol. in 2. Dublin, 1964.

――― *Na Manaigh Liatha in Éirinn*, Dublin, 1959.

――― 'Socio-economic Problems of the Late Medieval Irish Town' in *The Town in Ireland* (Historical Studies XIII) Ed. D. Harkness & M. O'Dowd. Belfast, 1981, pp 7-21.

McSkimin, Samuel. *The History and Antiquity of the county and the town of Carrickfergus.* Belfast, 1823.

Malden, H. E. (ed.). *The Cely Papers, Selections from the correspondence and memoranda of the Cely family, merchants of the staple, A.D. 1475-1488.* Camden Society, London, 1900.

Martin, G. H. and McIntyre, Sylvia. *A bibliography of British and Irish municipal history.* Leicester, 1972.

Maxwell, Constantia. *Irish history from contemporary sources. (1509-1610)* London, 1923.

Megaw. B. R. S. 'The Irish Shaggy Mantle' in *Jn. of the Manx Museum,* vol 5 (1945-6), p. 175.

Mitchell, Frank. *The Shell Guide to reading the Irish Landscape,* Dublin, 1986.

Mollat, Michel. *Le Commerce Maritime norman a la fin du moyen age.* Paris, 1952.

Moody, T. W. and Martin, F.X. *The Course of Irish History.* Cork, 1967.

—— and Byrne, F. J., (eds.) *A New History of Ireland, III-Early Modern Ireland, 1534-1691.* Oxford, 1976.

Mooney, Canice. 'Franciscan architecture in pre-Reformation Ireland'. In *R.S.A.I. Jn.,* lxxxvi (1956), pp 125-69.

Mullin, T. H. *Coleraine in bygone centuries.* Belfast, 1976.

Munro, H. A. *Wool, Cloth and Gold — the struggle for Bullion in Anglo-Burgundian Trade 1340-1478* Toronto, 1972.

Nicholls, Kenneth. *Gaelic and gaelicised Ireland in the middle ages.* Dublin, 1972.

—— 'Gaelic Society and Economy in the High Middle Ages'. In *N.H.I.,* II, pp 397-438.

Nicholson, R. G. 'An Irish Expedition to Scotland in 1335'. In *I.H.S.,* XIII (1962-3), pp 197-211.

O'Brien, A. F. 'The Development of the privileges, liberties and immunities of medieval Cork and the growth of an urban autonomy *c.* 1189-1500'. In *Cork Hist. Soc.Jn.,* XC (1985), pp 46-64.

Ó Cathain, Seán, 'Galway: historic outline 1169-1642'. In *Studies,* xxxi (1942), pp 456-466.

O'Donovan, John. *The Economic history of livestock in Ireland.* Cork, 1940.

O'Flaherty, Roderic. *A chorographical description of West or Iar Connaught, written A.D. 1684. Ed.* James Hardiman. Dublin, 1846. reprint Galway, 1977.

Ó Néill, Seamus. 'Irish maritime history: Early period to Norse invasions' in *Studies,* xxxiv (1945), pp 404-411.

Origo, Iris. *The Merchant of Prato- Francesco di Marco Datini.* Middlesex, 1963.

Orme, A.R. 'Youhgal, county Cork: growth, decay, resurgence' in *Irish Geography,* v. no. 3 (1966), pp 121-49.

Orpen. G. H. *Ireland under the Normans.* 4 vols, Oxford, 1911.

O'Sullivan, M. D.*Old Galway: the history of a Norman colony in Ireland.* Canbridge, 1942.

—— *Italian Merchant bankers in Ireland in the thirteenth century.* Dublin, 1962.

―――― 'Some Italian merchant bankers in Ireland in the late thirteenth century'. In *R.S.A.I. Jn.*, lxxix (1949), pp 10-19.

O'Sullivan, William. *The Economic history of Cork city from the earliest times to the Act of Union.* Cork, 1937.

Otway-Ruthven, A. J. *A History of Medieval Ireland.* London, 1968.

―――― 'The organisation of Anglo-Irish agriculture in the middle ages'. In *R.S.A.I. Jn.*, lxxxi (1951), pp 1-13.

Pearse, Richard. *The ports and harbours of Cornwall: an introduction to the study of 800 years of maritime affairs.* St. Austell, 1963.

Perry, R. 'The Gloucestershire woollen industry, 1100-1690'. In *Trans. Bristol and Gloucestershire Archaeological Society*, 1954, pp 49-137.

Platt, Colin. *Medieval Southampton — the port and trading community, 1200-1600.* London, 1973.

Pounds, N. J. G. 'The ports of Cornwall in the middle ages'. In *Devon and Cornwall notes and queries*, xxiii (1947-9), pp 65-73.

Power, Eileen and Postan, M. M. *Studies in English trade in the fifteenth century.* London, 1933.

Power, Rev. Prof. 'On a find of ancient jars in Cork City'. In *Cork Hist. Soc. Jn.*, xxxiii (1928), pp 10-11.

Power, Eileen. *The Wool Trade in English medieval History.* Oxford, 1941.

Powick, F. M. and Fryde, E. G. *Handbook of British Chronology.* Royal Historical Society, London, 1961.

Prendergast, P. 'Of hawks and hounds in Ireland'. In *R.S.A.I. Jn.*, ii (1852), pp 144-155.

Quinn, D. B. 'Guide to English financial records for Irish history, 1461-1588, with illustrative extracts, 1461-1509'. In *Anal. Hib.*, x (1941), pp 1-69.

―――― *Ulster, 1460-1550. Belfast, 1935. (reprinted from Belfast Natur. Hist. Soc. Proc.*, 1933-4).

Rees, William. *South Wales and the Marches 1284-1415; a social and agrarian study.* London, 1924.

Richardson, H. G. and Sayles, G.O. 'Irish Revenue, 1278-1384'. In *R.I.A. Proc.*, lxii, sect. c, (1961-3), pp 87-100.

Roberts, R. O. 'The Mills of Anglesey'. In *Trans. Anglesey Antiquarian Society.* 1958, p. 5.

Salzman, L. F. *English Trade in the Middle Ages.* London, 1964.

Scandurra, E. 'Medieval and renaissance ships in Italy' in *A history of seafaring, based on underwater archaeology.* ed. G. F. Bass. London, 1972.

'Sean-Ghall' 'Food control in medieval Ireland' in *Irish Theologial Quarterly*, xiii (1918), pp 105-112.

Simms, Katherine. 'The King's Friend': O'Neill, the Crown and the Earldom of Ulster'. In Lydon, *Eng.and Ire.*, Dublin, 1981.

―――― '*Guesting and Feasting in Gaelic Ireland' in R.S.A.I. Jn.*, cviii (1978) pp 67-100.

Smith, Charles. *The antient and present state of the county and town of Cork.* 2 vols. Dublin, 1750.

―――― *The antient and present state of the county of Kerry.* Dublin, 1756.

157

BIBLIOGRAPHY

Stalley, R.A. 'William of Prene and the Royal Works in Ireland' in *Journal of British Archaeological Assoc*, cxxxi (1978), pp 30-49.

Stanford-Reid, W. 'Sea-power in the Anglo-Scottish war 1296-1328'. In *The Mariner's Mirror*, xlvi (1960), pp 7-23.

—— 'Trade, Traders and Scottish Independence'. In *Speculum*, xxix (1954), pp 210-22.

Stephens, W. B. *Sources for English local history*. Manchester, 1973.

Swan, A. B. 'The port of Dundalk'. In *Louth Arch. Soc. Jn.*, xvii (1970), pp 66-78.

Taylor, E. G. R. *The haven-finding Art — A History of Navigation from Odysseus to Captain Cook*. London, 1971.

Thrupp, Sylvia. 'A Survey of the alien population of England in 1440. In *Speculum*, xxxii (1957), pp 262-73.

Touchard, Henri. *Le commerce maritime breton a la fin du moyen age*. Paris, 1967.

Unger, R. W. *The Ship in the Medieval Economy, 600-1600*. London and Montreal, 1980.

Veale, E. M. *The English fur trade in the later middle ages*. Oxford, 1966.

Waterman, D. M. 'Medieval pottery from Nendrum and Grey Abbey'. In *Ulster Journal of Archaeology*, xxi, 3 (1958), pp 67-73.

—— 'Somersetshire and other foreign building stone in medieval Ireland *c.* 1175-1400'. In *Ulster Journal of Archaeology*, xxxiii, 3 (1970), pp 63-75.

Watt, J. A. 'Approaches to the history of fourteenth century Ireland'. In *N.H.I.* II, pp 303-313.

Wood, Herbert. 'Commercial intercourse with Ireland in the middle ages'. In *Studies*, iv (1915), pp 250-266.

Went, A. E. J. 'Eel fishing at Athlone, past and present'. In *R.S.A.I. Jn.*, lxxx (1950), pp 146-154.

—— 'The fisheries of the river Boyne'. In *Louth Arch. Soc. Jn.*, xiii (1953), pp 18-33.

—— 'Fisheries of the river Liffey: notes on the corporation fishery up to the dissolution of the monasteries'. In *R.S.A.I. Jn.*, lxxxiii (1953), pp 163-173.

—— 'The fisheries of the Munster Blackwater'. In *R.S.A.I. Jn.*, xc (1960), pp 97-131, continued in xci (1961), pp 19-41.

—— 'Fishing weirs on the river Erne'. In *R.S.A.I. Jn.*, lxxv (1945), pp 213-23.

—— 'The Galway fishery, an account of the ownership of the fishery'. In *R.I.A. Proc.*, xlix, sect. c (1943 -4), pp 187-219.

—— 'Historical notes on some of the fisheries of Co. Louth'. In *Louth Arch. Soc. Jn.*, xiv, no. 3 (1959), pp 178-190.

—— 'Historical notes on the fisheries of the river Suir'. In *R.S.A.I. Jn.*, lxxxvi (1956), pp 192-202.

—— 'Historical notes on the fisheries of the two county Sligo rivers'. In *R.S.A.I. Jn.*, xcix (1969), pp 55-61.

—— 'The Irish hake fishery, 1504-1824'. In *Cork Hist. Soc. Jn.*, li (1946), pp41-51.

—— 'Irish monastic fisheries'. In *Cork Hist. Soc. Jn.*, lx (1955), pp 47-56.

—— 'The Ling in Irish commerce'. In *R.S.A.I. Jn.*, lxxviii (1948), pp 119-126.

—— 'The pursuit of salmon in Ireland'. In *R.I.A. Proc*, lxiii, sect. c (1962-4), pp 191-244.

—— "A short history of the fisheries of the river Nore'. In *R.S.A.I. Jn.*, lxxv (1955), pp 22-33.

Westropp, T. J. 'Early Italian maps of Ireland from 1300 to 1600 with notes on foreign settlers and trade'. In *R.I.A. Proc.*, xxx, sect. c (1913), pp 361-428.

Wilson, R. P. The port of Chester in the later middle ages (Ph.D. thesis, University of Liverpool, 1965).

——— 'The port of Chester in the fifteenth century' in *Trans. of the Hist. Soc. of Lancashire and Cheshire*, cxvii (1965), pp 1-15.

Younge, C. M. 'Fisheries in History: The Tunny, the Herring and the Cod; in *History Today*, xxv (1975).

Index

almonds 96
armour 91
Arthur, Thomas 65, 76, 82

balingers 109
Bardi, the 62
barges 109
barley 20
barrels 102
Bataille, John de la 52-4
Bayonne 45, 46
beans 29
Bigod, Roger 59
birds of prey 98, 102-3
Blake family 56, 67, 71, 82
  John Oge 82, 90
Bordeaux 44-6
Bourgneuf Bay 51, 84, 86
Boys, Richard 72, 75
Bristol 28, 29, 60-1, 103
  cloth trade 66, 71-2
  fish trade 35, 38-40
  salt trade 86, 88
  ships from 108-10
Brittany 49, 84-5, 104-5
  piracy 84-5, 122-5
Butler family 51-2, 96, 111

Calais 80, 109
  staple 60, 63-4, 78, 85
caravels 110-11
carracks 109-10
Carrickfergus 24-5
Chester 23, 27-8, 60, 90
  cloth trade 72-4
  fish trade 31, 40-1

hides trade 78
skins trade 98-9
Church(e), John 78, 128
cloth production 65-76
  English trade 70-4
  linen 67-8
  mantles 68-9
  sale and distribution 74-6
coal 100
cocket, letters of 63, 71, 77-8, 79
cod 36-7
cogs 107-8
Cork 26-7, 62, 63, 112
corn 20-9
  export of 21-3, 27-9
  internal trade 23-7
  purveyance of 22-3, 29
  scarcity 29
Coventry 60, 72-3, 99
crannock, definition of 22
crayers 111-12
crop rotation 20, 58
customs revenue 45, 77, 78, 101
  Great Custom 58-9

Dartas, Janico 90, 112, 124
de Burgh, Elizabeth 40
de Burgo family 47-8, 51, 80, 90, 127
de Moenes, Robert 89-90, 91
Drogheda 31, 79, 87
  piracy 122
  salt trade 85-6
  shipbuilding 112, 121
  staple 62, 63
Dublin 52, 66, 74, 80

staple 62, 63
Dublin Castle 92, 93, 94
Dundry oolite 92
dyes 65-6, 70

Edward I 20, 23, 44, 45, 58-9, 101, 119
Edward II 47, 118, 119
Edward III 103
Edward IV 75
eels 37, 41-2

faldings 68-9
fish trade 30-43, 46-7, 112
  freshwater fish 37-42
  herrings 30-6
  tithes 34, 43

Flanders 68, 77, 78-9
  wool trade 59-60, 64
forestallers 31-2
Frescobaldi, the 45, 59, 62, 92
frieze (serge) 60, 66-7
fruit 96-7
furs 98

Gaelic Irish 36, 90, 99-100, 121
  arms 91
  corn trade 24, 26
  crafts 95-6
  hides 80-1
  horses 104, 106
  ships 91, 112, 121
Galway 39, 63, 80-1
  piracy 127-8
  wine trade 48-9
Gascony 22-3, 28, 78
  wine trade 44-51
Giraldus Cambrensis 29, 44, 117
goldsmiths 95-6
Great Custom 58-9
guilds 74, 131

hake 37

Hanseatic League 30, 60, 66, 77, 84, 108, 116, 118
hawks 98, 102-3
Henry II 96, 97
Henry IV 103
Henry V 98
Henry VI 73
Henry VII 64, 94
Henry VIII 32, 103, 125, 131
herring fisheries 30-7, 131
  Atlantic 33-5
  Irish Sea 31-3
hides trade 39, 45, 46, 63, 77-83
  prices 80-1
hobelars 104
honey 96
horses 104-6
hulks 108
Hundred Years' War 50, 55, 62, 63

iron trade 84-7, 90-1
Isle of Man 118, 121, 124
Italian bankers 44, 45, 58-60
  merchants 94-5

Ken(e)feg, Ralph 84, 104-5
Kinsale 26, 35, 112, 126, 128-9

Lambay Island 125
last, definition of 39
lead 93
licences
  corn 21-2, 28
  fish 33, 38-9
Limerick 29, 49
  piracy 128
linen 67-8
Lombards 74
London
  cloth trade 73

mantles 68-70
marten skins 98
merchants 21, 74, 79, 80, 131
  English 74-5

salt trade 89-90
shipping attacked 126-9
wine trade 45-51
millstones 92
monasteries 21, 59
fisheries 36-8, 43
wool trade 58, 59
Mustard, Thomas 47, 61

navigation 113-16
Noe, Maurice de la 29, 96

oats 20
olive oil 97
O'Malley family 80, 127
oysters 41

pack, definition of 39
pickards 111-12
piracy 50-1, 84-5, 119-29
Breton and Spanish 84-5, 109, 122-6
Scots 119-21
ships used 109, 111
Portugal 48-9, 114
portulan maps 114, 119
pottery 90-1
pots and pans 91
prise of wine 51-2
purveyance
corn 22, 27
wine 44, 55

Riccardi, the 59, 62, 96
Richard II 23, 98, 103
river fisheries 37-42
river freight 55-6, 61, 80, 92, 99
rutters 114-16

salmon 37-41
salt trade 84-90
Spain 86-8
Scotland 23-4, 61-2
piracy 119-21
sea travel, hazards of 50, 117-19, 126-9

Semeonis, Symon 118-19
ships, types of 107-112
building of 112-13
numbers 113
wrecks 116-19
shoemaking 81-2
silk 94-5
silversmiths 95
skins 98-9
Spain 34, 86, 88
piracy 122-6
wine trade 48-9, 52, 114
spices 96
staple, statute of 85
Statute of Westminster 116
stone 92-3
Symcock, William 27, 40, 46, 112

tillage 20-1, 29, 58
timber 99-102
export of 100-2
Tregury, Abp Michael 95, 117-18, 124-5
turf 100

Ulster 24, 56, 121

vestments 94-5

Waterford 55, 61, 79
cloth trade 69-71
defence of 91, 122
charter 95
Gaelic trade 80, 91
salt trade 88-9
staple 63, 64
wax 97
weapons 91
weirs 37-8, 41-2
Welles, James 68, 74, 75
wheat 20
Wilde, John 68, 72
wine trade 28, 39, 44-57
costs 52-4, 57
distribution 54-7
France 44-8

prise 51-2
Spain and Portugal 48-9
wool trade 58-64
staple 62-4

wrecks 116-19

Ylane, James 121-2